EILEEN
A Chronicle of Memories Over 100 years

Eileen Zwettler Harrington

Fancy Gram Books—Mineral Point, WI
ISBN: 979-8-9881299-0-5
eBook ISBN: 979-8-9881299-1-2
Title: *Eileen: A Chronicle of Memories Over 100 years*
Author: Eileen Zwettler Harrington
Digital distribution | 2023
Paperback | 2023

Dedication

In memory of my loving parents, Joseph and Mary.

Foreword

Hello, Reader! My siblings and I are grateful you have chosen to read Mom's recollections of her family members' lives' journeys. You will find excerpts to be historic, some hilarious, and others heartbreaking. Of note, in typing her handwritten booklets of each family member, I have tried to keep the language true to form as she had written them when she was the age of ninety-three. When Mom's eyesight began to deteriorate from macular degeneration and glaucoma after her ninety-fifth birthday, I began writing her dictated stories and anecdotes in a loose leaf binder filling numerous pages. Oftentimes, these stories would flow as Mom and many of us, family members and friends, would be playing cards in her basement rec room sitting around the poker table. Someone would remark, "Is that in the book?" A quick note would be scribbled on a napkin, score pad, piece of junk mail and placed in the binder to be retold at a later date. The task of assembling the booklets and binder pages took a few months and every time I thought Mom's book complete, there would be something new to add. It was a life lesson in the works to know…that there is always one more story!

Nancy Harrington Harker

Chapter One
Joseph and Mary

This is the history of the lives of Joseph and Mary Zwettler and their children, as penned by the youngest of the ten, Eileen Eleanor Zwettler Harrington.

My grandparents were immigrants. Dad's father, Florian, was born in Iamboe (in 1900 changed to Eulanbach), Austria on April 26, 1844. When he was twenty-six years old he boarded the steamship, Berlin, at Bremen on May 23, 1870 with 661 other passengers and a crew numbering eighteen headed for America. Florian met Agnes Litschaur from Rohrbach, Austria on the steamship. They were later married in Cross Plains, Wisconsin on August 21,1870. They settled in Vermont Township for a short time then went to Chicago where Florian worked as a carpenter after the Great Chicago Fire in October of 1871. After a year there, they moved back to Vermont where they farmed for many years. He built the pews for the first Catholic church in Vermont Township. Florian and Agnes never mastered the English language. They would use German words when they couldn't recall the English ones!

Dad (Joe) had three brothers: Tom (Nellie Torphy), Chris (Rose Handel), Frank (Alice Boyle) - and three sisters, Theresa (Joe Gabalt), Mary (Dan Lynch) & Agnes (who later went to the convent and took the title Sr. Isabelle in the Dominican order in Racine, Wisconsin. Sr. Isabelle had many degrees in teaching and at one time taught school in Sauk City. One of her students was August Durleth, noted writer and author.

When Agnes passed away on November 26, 1918, Florian lived with his son-in-law and daughter Dan and Mary Lynch for a year then with his daughter Theresa Gabalt. He was blind the final eleven years of his life and partially paralyzed from a stroke. His obituary in 1927 said, "Death came to him as a relief..." Florian and Agnes are now interred in the Catholic cemetery in Mount Horeb.

Mom's parents were Peter Von Bergen (born in Meiringen, Switzerlandand, December 26, 1830) and Rosina Wyler (born March 27, 1847 at Horgen, Zurich, Switzerland). Rosina came from a large family of fourteen siblings and she was about twenty years younger than Peter. They were married in March of 1875. Peter was a wagonmaker and shoemaker in Switzerland but was driven out of business with the advent of machines. Peter, Rosina and family came to America by steamship thinking of settling in Ohio. Mom (Mary) was only three years old. However, while aboard, they heard about work in coal mines of Pennsylvania. They settled in Taylor, Pennsylvania where her dad and brothers worked in the coal mines. Rosina was a midwife at the time and knew much about herbs.

Mom had two brothers, Casper and Peter, and two sisters, Rose and Bertha. Bertha was born in the United States. Peter and Rosina also took in a little boy of Mary's sister named Albert. Sadly, Albert died when he was almost three years old. Her father, Peter, supposedly died from coal dust but a story endures that he was taken ill and was given the wrong prescription of saltpeter instead of epsom salts. He died in 1893 and was buried in Taylor, Pennsylvania. Her mother moved the remaining family to Wisconsin.

Dad was born on July 21, 1878 and grew up on a farm on Zwettler Road outside of Blue Mounds. I believe he attended grade school completing all eight grades. He was very bright and talented. Dad loved to dance and often went to the Opera House in Blue Mounds. Dad could call square dances. Mom also had a great love of music and dancing and often went to the Opera House. She was a black raven beauty with almost black eyes. Dad was very smitten with her. He said when he saw her, "There is my wife!" And the saga begins.

The union began when Joseph and Mary married on February 25, 1905 and bought a 188 acre farm in the Cross Plains Township in the Pine Bluff area on County Trunk J. It consisted of an old house, barn, and chicken house. In 1905 there was no electricity in the country. You lived by kerosene lamps and lanterns with a pump in the house for water and we used outside toilets. The house had a front porch and you entered into the dining room which had a round cast iron heater. Off to the right was a bedroom, to the left was the parlor. Off that parlor was another bedroom. You went straight through the dining room to get to the kitchen which had a wood stove. Off the kitchen was a washroom that had a wringer washer. There were two large bedrooms upstairs reached by a stairway off the right side of the dining room.

Besides operating our farm in Wisconsin, to make ends meet, Dad sharecropped a farm in South Dakota and he would take machinery back and forth on the train. By that time some of my siblings were old enough to help manage farm chores here while Dad was working there.

Looking toward the future, Dad built a big barn about a quarter mile from the existing buildings about in the center of the 188 acres. A well was dug with a windmill and cistern for water. Dad piped water to the barn, didn't he use his head?! After completion of the barn, a beautiful house was erected. A porch the width of the house faced the road. You entered into a large living room. Mom had beautiful furniture and draperies. Off to the right was a large bedroom and on the door was a full-length mirror. Mom liked to pose in front of it, she was pretty fashionable! Straight through the living room through french doors was the dining room. Dad built a beautiful hutch along the whole wall of the right side. There was a big kitchen, pantry and stairway off the dining room. The open stairway had six steps to a landing. You could go up one direction to the bedrooms, the other direction down to Mom and Dad's closet in their bedroom. The upstairs consisted of three bedrooms: a small one to the left where opposite was a bathroom (toilet, bathtub, and linen closet), the other bedrooms were down the hall. One big, huge mistake was that only one bedroom had a closet! At the end of the hallway was a porch. Marie used to lay out there to get a suntan - with not much on! There was also a huge attic and full basement.

The home was heated by a wood furnace. Because there was no electricity Dad built his own generator in the basement. It was huge in one corner with many steel pieces. Dad had a brilliant mind to figure that out! After a few years of living on the new place, Dad took up a petition with the neighbors for an electricity line to be erected in the country road and eventually it was passed by the county board so the plant in the basement of the house could be disposed of.

My earliest recollection of moving to our new home was when Ray (my brother who was two years older) and I sat on top of the chicken house when it was moved to the new farm.

It was a beautiful farm; one you were proud to bring your friends home to. There were many Zwettler reunions and other family/friends gatherings there. One such incidental gathering made the papers! One fall, an old neighbor, Bill Meicher from Sauk City, came and asked Dad if he could build a still in the basement. Dad agreed! That winter, a wicked snow storm blew in and you couldn't even travel on the roads. Farmers had to open fence lines and go through fields. Drifts were as high as telephone poles and caterpillars had to come to open roads. Around midnight, the drivers stopped at our farm to get warm and were offered booze. Their wives turned Dad in and the sheriff came and asked to enter the house. He found the still and Dad was fined $75. My sister, Marie, was teaching at the Murphy School and she paid the fine. She only made $75 a month! My brother, Leo, was a barber in Baraboo at the time and a customer waiting in a chair was reading a Madison paper and read aloud the article about a sheriff finding a still at Joe Zwettler's farm. Leo went berserk, left the customer in the chair and went home to the farm. Leo was furious with Dad and Dad just responded, "He was a family friend and I never thought we'd be caught. It was for our own use!" (Eileen- "It was good!" The leftover liquid from making alcohol called "kimmel" was clear like water!")

My mother was a hard working resourceful woman, she raised ten children! When first married she did housework in Mazomanie and knew Margaret Sweeney (who would later become my mother-in-law). She always had her own horse and buggy to go to town. Mom talked about working for a neighbor on the Fourth of July picking potato bugs and watching cars going by to the big parade. Isn't that pathetic! She had so much patience. Her housekeeping was meticulous and her meals nutritious and delicious. You had to eat what you had in the house. Dad always butchered a beef and two pigs at the same time. It would be cut up in the basement of the house. Mom made homemade sausage (which I had a hard time eating because we cleaned the intestines to use as the casing), canned meat, and "side meat" which was fried until crisp and layered in a huge crock with lard. It never spoiled. She also made quarts upon quarts of dill pickles and bought Michigan peaches to can. They were the best! Dad cured hams in a wood shed and when they were done, he wrapped them in burlap to hang in the basement. We lived on karo syrup, Mom bought it by the pail. We would put it on pancakes, cottage cheese, toast, fried cornbread, etc. When the pails were empty, we kids used them for lunch buckets.

Christmas at the farm was a big event. Mama went all out for this holiday. Dad or whoever was home went out to the woods to cut down a tree. One year Ray and Bernard were in charge of putting the tinsel on the tree. They began very deliberately, one tinsel piece at a time but ended up just throwing clumps helter skelter all over from top to bottom. All the family that were working would come with clothes baskets full of gifts. Our favorite recipe was the poppy seed noodles made from bread dough. (Recipe is included!) On Christmas Eve, after the boys were done milking, we had the warm noodles and prune sauce. Dad requested the prunes because he thought all that dough made one constipated! Everyone went to Midnight Mass and would come home, fire up the stove, reheat the noodles and continue to visit. As people married into the family it was always a wonder if they'd like the noodles. Most of the in-laws did- Jack, Leah, Lois, and Doris. Doris even learned how to make them for Ray. Todd didn't like them and even commented, "Thank God for the coffee to get them down!"

Mom was a very devout convert to the Catholic faith. During Lent, she made all of us kneel beside the dining room chairs to say the Rosary. Dad knew all the mysteries and kept us in line. In one of Mom's religious books she read about the Blessed Virgin's request at Fatima that if one confessed sins, recited the Rosary, went to Mass and received communion on the First Saturdays of five consecutive months, She would assist at the hour of death. Our mother suffered through several physical ailments. She lived with pernicious anemia that oftentimes made her fatigued. and she required B12 shots later in life. When she was in her forties she needed an appendectomy which was performed on the kitchen table! Her brother, Pete, had to hold her on the table as well as administer chloroform. He overheard one doctor say, "Did you cut the intestine? The other responded, "No, I didn't, did you?"

Mom had a terrible accident in the early 1930s when I was about eight or nine years old. In the fall of the year, Mom decided to start a fire in the furnace in the basement by lighting the kindling so it would be warm for us when we got home from school. In the process there was an explosion and Mom's right hand was injured plus she suffered cuts on her face. She managed to get upstairs to call Mary Meicher for help. The telephone was a wall phone with a crank and it was a labor to use her left hand. When she reached Mary she said, "Mary, come quick, I'm hurt!!" A close neighbor, Henrietta Laufenberg "rubbered" on the phone and immediately went to get her husband Tony to help. They took Mom to the doctor in Mount Horeb. The tendons in her hand were severely injured but they stitched what they could and bound her hand in a curved form. That night she sat in a rocker with a catalog under her bound hand and would turn the pages as they became saturated with blood. My sister, Grace, was called home from Madison to care for her and would turn the pages as the pain was so great. Several days later, my dad was putting wood in the furnace and found dynamite caps in the chunks of wood. (He had hired someone to cut lumber in the woods and that person had used dynamite caps.) If Mom hadn't been wearing glasses, she would have been blinded. She never wore glasses regularly but she was sewing at the time and forgot to take them off. When I got home from school, Mary Meicher was scrubbing the blood off the floor. Mom lived her life with a crippled right hand. She learned to hold utensils and could even hold a pencil to write.

Grandma Bergen was living in Kansas with another daughter, Aunt Rose Zalzman, when Mom got a call her mother was very ill and not expected to live. Mom, with baby John who was six weeks old, took the train to Kansas. Her mom was not a member of any church at the time and Mom asked her if she wanted to see a priest (Mom was a convert). A priest was called, she became a Catholic on her deathbed and Dad paid all funeral expenses from Kansas to Wisconsin and buried her in the Zwettler plot. I don't know how Dad afforded all they had and did! He even bought eighty acres for his sister and brother-in-law (Theresa and Joe Gabalt) in Pine Bluff! He paid for a dressmaker, Lizzy Schaeffer, to come and stay at the farm to sew dresses for the girls.

Mom was ill off and on and Grace would have to quit her job and come home to help until she got better. I think she suffered periods of depression. During this time a lady from Mazomanie came to clean the house *for Mom. Mom's beautiful dishes and other items started to disappear! There were some missing antique plates plus a favorite china tea set Helen had bought for Mom. Years later I went to a garage sale at this lady's house and low and behold....there was Mom's recipe book! I never asked about the other items, what good would come of that!*

When mother's health began failing, they sold the farm and moved to Madison to share a home with Isabelle (my oldest sister) on the west side of the city. They lived there several years when Mom became very ill in April of 1963. I knew about her devotion to the Blessed Virgin and I believe she saw her moments before death, for she smiled! Dad was healthy and never in a hospital up to the time he got pneumonia, and a few days later, died at the age of ninety-two in December of 1969.

Just a side note: Dad sold the farm in the year of 1959 to a neighbor who always wanted it for the price of $38,000. Many years later the farm was sold again for $348,000 to some doctor in Madison.

(Von) Bergen Family
Rose, Peter, Casper
Bertha, Mary, Rosina

Zwettler Children
Mary, Agnes, Theresa
Joseph, Tom, Chris
Frank, Marita (died as a youngster)

4

Zwettler Family

Joseph Z., Frank Z., Theresa Z.(Gabalt), Sister Isabel, Mary Z.(Lynch), Tom Z., Chris Z. Grace, Mary (holding Leo), Florian Z., Isabel, Agnes Z., Anna, Rose (m. Chris) , Margaret

Joe, Tom, Mary, Sister Isabel, Frank, Theresa

Sister Isabel

Mary and Joseph's Engagement Picture

Joseph

Joseph and Mary's Wedding Picture

Joseph and Mary's Fiftieth Wedding Anniversary

Chapter Two
Isabel (The Rock)

*I*sabel was born September 18th of 1906. I am certain being the oldest of ten children, she was a huge help in raising the clan. She went to school until the eighth grade but didn't continue onto high school. She was seventeen years of age and on a date to a barn dance the night I was born. When I was six years old, she married Virgil Lucey of Mazomanie where he farmed on Matthewson Road for twelve years. Isabel loved being a farmwife. Her saddest day happened in the fall of 1940 when Virgil was diagnosed with an inoperable brain tumor. The doctors at St. Mary's referred him to University Hospital. At University, he was offered no hope. She wanted the best for him so with Virgil's two brothers, Wilfred and Leo, they traveled to Mayo Clinic in Minnesota. Driving Isabel and Virgil's new car over the viaduct in Mazomanie, he exclaimed, "I'll never see Mary Ellen (their daughter) grow up!" Then on the way to Minneapolis they stopped at his sister Nan and Peter Hettingter's home and while he was there, he went blind. He died at Mayo Hospital on December 19, 1941. The wake for Virgil was at their house and I can remember Mary Ellen running around. In his memory, Isabel bought a chalice (monstrom) and gave it to St. Barnabas Church in Mazomanie. It is still there.

They had adopted a baby girl, Mary Ellen, in January of 1936 so she was about the age of four when her dad passed away. Because there was no one to operate the farm, Isabel sold their personal property (the mother-in-law would never sell the farm to Virgil) but when it had to be sold, Isabel moved to Mazomanie with Virgil's mother until she passed away. Isabel then moved to Madison on North Franklin Street. She bought a house about five blocks from the capital and rented out rooms to male boarders. One was a university professor who treated Isabel to dinner and university affairs. When he was offered a position in Walla Walla Washington, he asked Isabel to marry him and make the move with him but she declined! I have the dainty china tea set he once gave her.

She had several menial jobs when first residing in Madison. One was operating a clean towel service. Helen Brandenmule, a close friend, was instrumental in her getting a job in a research lab working with rat brains at University Hospital. She had to wear a white lab coat every day, which she probably loved! She worked there for many years until her retirement. They threw a huge retirement party for her! Afterwards, they would call her frequently with questions. She had a good retirement!

In the meantime, when our mom's health failed, she sold her home and shared a home with them on Sprague Street on the west side of Madison. Then Mom passed away in April of 1963 and then Dad lived there until his death in December of 1969.

Isabel was very dedicated to her job at the lab but in 1975 when she had retired, she sold her house on Sprague Street that she had inherited from her mom and dad and moved into an apartment at the Tower Hills Apartments (across from the Department of Motor Vehicles). She was our rock. Sometimes she called me three times a day when she moved to the apartment. At that time she was in her seventies and would take our sister, Helen, all over Madison doing her errands. The problem was finding a route because Isabel could only make right turns!

She had a traumatic event in 1990 which changed her life! Mary Ellen (daughter) and Graham (son-in-law) showed up at her apartment with their son, Ben. They expected Isabel to board him while he was going to UW-Madison. Isabel could never understand their lack of consideration because they were educated people! Mary Ellen had a degree in early childhood education and Graham was a professor of law. I never heard Isabel cry so hard as she did when she called to tell me about it. It truly stressed her to the point where it affected her thinking.

She resided there until March of 1994, when she became ill with the beginning of dementia and couldn't be alone so I had to put her in a nursing home. I chose the Greenway Manor in Spring Green simply because brother Ray and his wife, Doris, also lived in the area. It's of interest that Isabel never had a hospital stay until she broke her hip falling in the nursing home. She must have had great faith in me because she made me her "Power of Attorney." Isabel had excellent care until February 2000 when she passed away at the age of ninety-four. She is buried by her husband Virgil in the Catholic cemetery in Mazomanie.

Sidenote: Mary Ellen and Graham died as wards of the state of Virginia!

Isabel's Baby Picture

Grace and Isabel

Grace, Leo, and Isabel

9

Murphy School

Grace and Isabel are in the first row to the right of the teacher.

Virgil, Peter and Nan Hettinger, Isabel

They were wedding attendants for the couple in the middle.

Mary Ellen's Class picture from UW-Madison

Chapter Three
Grace (Beloved)

*G*race was born on November 5, 1907. When I was born she was sixteen years old. There was a neighbor girl the same age and was so jealous that Isabel & Grace had a "little doll" (me) to take care of. Grace was a petite little thing, 5ft 2 inches tall, a sweet disposition much like brother Ray and was easy to get along with. She enjoyed being in the kitchen helping Mom. Whereas Isabel hated housekeeping; if there was any sewing to do that was more her interest. Grace got her period when she was six years old and it stunted her growth. She only wore a size six shoe!

Grace never went to high school. She had friends who worked in dormitories at the University of Wisconsin so they convinced her, with her culinary skills, to apply. She got the job and was much in demand in the kitchens. Her pies were to die for!!! She also was employed at different restaurants in the area. One was owned by a woman named Agnes and hired Grace to open up in the mornings. On Saturdays, I would help when UW football games were held doing waitress work and Agnes took care of the cash register. I never got paid, just helped out.

Agnes had an ex-husband, Charles, who had a jewelry store one block off the square. Grace volunteered me to help so I wound up working at the counter. I was given the task of ordering jewelry out of catalogs and pricing them when delivered. Can you imagine that?? I loved it but again I wasn't paid!! An interesting thing about Agnes and Charles was that though they were divorced, they shared a great big house. Agnes even had a boyfriend!

Grace didn't date much; one boyfriend I remember was a short chubby real estate man. He'd come to the farm to see her when she was home on a weekend. They'd usually go to a movie in Mt. Horeb. Once when watching a picture starring Joan Fontaine, he told Grace he saw a great resemblance between Miss Fontaine and Eileen!

When America was bombed at Pearl Harbor on Dec. 7, 1941 and we were declared at war, Army bases were installed all over the country. It was at Truax Field in Madison where Grace met her future husband and soldier, John Hammond. He was from Enigma, Georgia, had one brother and his mother owned a grocery with a dirt floor. After marriage, that's what she went home to. They shared a bedroom off the store floor with his mother.

They began traveling base to base. Before their first child was born they were at an armed base in Mexico. John wanted a safer birth place in a hospital so he sent Grace back to Dodgeville, Wisconsin to stay with our sister, Helen, and brother-in-law, Todd. Their first child was a son, Jack ("Jackie", my godson) and when he was a few weeks old they returned to John. When John was sent to an army base in Kansas, Isabel and I went to see them at their apartment. I never liked John and I told him right to his face that Grace was too good for him! He straightened out and was a good dad. They finally settled in Warner Robins, Georgia.

When Jackie was three years old, John spent all his days at the pool hall and had no employment. At 3:00 AM one morning, Grace was packing a suitcase to leave him when he came home. John was alarmed and called a close friend named Pete and said he needed a job. Pete took him to a place in Warner Robins where he got a job in a "motor pool." Whatever the devil a motor pool was, I'd like to know! I know this happened for a fact because later in life I was visiting Grace and stayed with a couple of her friends, Pete and Lou. They told me the whole story!

It was heartbreaking for Grace when she miscarried a baby girl at four months. John saw the baby and she was terribly deformed and didn't want Grace to see her. She devoted her whole life to Jackie. He was a handsome, quiet, talented boy. He excelled in baseball in high school and the New York Yankees scouted him and wanted to sign him. John wouldn't sign for him because he thought it necessary for Jackie to get an education. Grace felt so sorry for her son for she knew then his baseball career was over. He went on to be an educator and principal. He has three sons, one who worked for the CIA and knew about the hunt for Osama Bin Laden!

Grace made many trips to Wisconsin, the early ones in a Model A Ford. She remained close to our family and was able to attend the funerals of Mom and Dad.

Grace suffered with arthritis for a number of years, lived to be in her eighties- with her health failing Jack put her in a nursing home until she passed away on August 30, 1997. Her husband was deceased and both are buried in Warner Robins. Sadly, her son Jack has passed and leaves behind a wife and 3 sons and seven grandchildren.

An afterthought: While working at one of the sororities, she befriended a family by the name of Jordan who had a teenage son- a spoiled brat. Many Sundays they would bring Grace out to the farm on a Sunday afternoon. On a particular Sunday Alex Jr. shot out a couple windows out of the barn with a sling shot! Dad was not too happy!!!

Many years later this same Alex Jordan was a builder and owner of the "House on the Rock"

Isabel and Grace

John, Jackie, and Grace

13

Mary, John, Grace, and Isabel

Grace and John

Jackie, Grace, and John

Chapter Four
Leo (Hollywood Handsome)

*L*eo was born on February 24, 1909. As expected he was my dad's pride and joy. From what Mom told me many times he followed Dad everywhere and as he grew older he was a great help in being a big brother to sisters, Isabel, Grace and Serene. Mom asked Leo once, why he hadn't ridden to town with Papa and he responded, "Cause you wouldn't watch Serene and that rooster would get her!"

Farming in his teenage years was not his "cup of tea"; milking cows, mucking cow and horse stalls, mowing hay and all daily chores was not in his future. One morning while hauling milk to the cheese factory he told the cheesemaker how unhappy he was on the farm and wanted to be a barber but there was no way financially he could afford to go on to school. Apparently the cheesemaker understood how much Leo wanted a change, he gave Leo the money to enroll in barber school in Milwaukee. After graduation he got a job in a barber shop in Baraboo. He rented a room in a private home of an elderly childless couple who, needless to say, adopted him (Mr. and Mrs. Farnsworth). They would often bring him home to the farm and Mom would always prepare a delicious meal for them.

Leo was "Hollywood Handsome" but his looks never went to his head. Brother Ray remembered going with him to Mt. Horeb, and while they were walking down the street a woman stopped and said aloud, "That's the most handsome man I've ever seen!" Leo , Helen and John were often taken for Italians because their coloring was so dark.

While working in Baraboo he met his future wife, Alea Hanson, who lived in a resort at the Wisconsin Dells. Her mother was a beautiful lady! Alea had a brother, Harold, and a sister, Ethyl (married Jim Donaldson). Mr. & Mrs. Hanson owned a resort at the Dells. Bandits came in to rob them. Mr. Hanson would not open the cash register and he was shot and killed. This preceded the meeting of Alea & Leo. While living in Baraboo, Leo and Alea had a son Lee and shortly after then moved to West Moreland Street in Madison. WWII was so bad at that time they had to enlist married men! Leo was drafted and went to Okinawa. A neighbor, Sylvia Farrell Vassen, once saw Alea out to dinner with a man while Leo was overseas. Our family knew Leo was the love of her life so nothing came of it.

Alea and Lee often stayed at the farm in Pine Bluff while Leo was away. My mom happened to be making sauerkraut on one of their visits. Mom told Lee, "You should eat a lot of sauerkraut because it's full of iron." Lee responded, " Daddy should eat it then so bullets won't go through him!" They had a second son, Billy. Lee and Billy were eleven months apart. As fate would have it, Billy was a Down syndrome baby. At eight months of age, their family doctor, social worker, and parish priest advised Leo & Alea to place Billy in a state institution in northern Wisconsin. At the age of thirty, he moved to Madison to a group home where he resided with the help of a caregiver until his death at the age of sixty. He is buried in the Hillside Cemetery in Madison.

In the year of 1947, Leo moved his family to Seattle where he managed the barber shop at the University of Washington. Leo had a staff of twenty barbers. He had not gone to high school but he could hob-nob with professors and speak to every subject! He was a staunch Democrat and could address his views with competence. While in Seattle they had a daughter, Katie, who now lives in California. When I asked Leo about his greatest sadness, he confessed it was when Katy became involved in a cult overseas. They couldn't find her for months and Alea was beside herself with worry. She would often pace the floors saying a rosary. Alea went to an ambassador for help and they found her! My son Steve heard Leo telling our brother, Ray, about it and how they had to send $50,000 to get her home! I think Katy was pampered, she was a great skier and Leo always wanted her to have the best! She became a family therapist and is an author.

In their later years, Leo always kept very close ties to his family in Wisconsin, making many trips home. He *missed Christmas Eve in Wisconsin- mostly the poppy seed noodles his mother would make AND the Christmas morning coffee cake. My daughter, Joan, had graduated from Dr. Scholl's in Chicago and during their visit to our farm in Arena, my daughter, Joan, made him a Black Russian. He loved it!! He really wasn't a drinker because he had a terrible ulcer and he had to carry orange juice in the car for his blood sugar. At Christmastime in 1987, Leo came to Madison with the family- Alea, Lee and Katy. He wanted to show Lee and Katy where he had the barbershop at UW-Wisconsin. He was dying from cancer. Over the course of that excursion, he told his children they had another brother with Down syndrome and he was eleven months younger than Lee. Alea went with Lee to meet him and as they walked away Lee said, "There but for the grace of God, go I!"*

Leo passed away on Jan 29, 1988 and Leah died on Feb 9, 1990. Leah had been on oxygen and when they found her, the mask was off! I think she just wanted to be with Leo! Their ashes were scattered in a park in Seattle! Their son, Lee, had a stroke and resided in a nursing home in California until his death.

Leo

Leo in Service

Lea and Leo's Engagement Picture

Leo and Lee

18

Lee, Leo and Katie in Madison WI.
Leo was ill with cancer and on this trip he told Lee and Katy they had a brother, Billy.

Chapter Five
Serene (Our Angel)

Serene was born on Aug 4, 1910. Leo & Serene were only two years apart and were great pals. He was her protector of a mean Leghorn rooster who would attack them in the play yard. When Serene was thirteen years old she was ill for two weeks with appendicitis, then taken to the hospital and had surgery for a ruptured appendix. She seemingly was improving after the surgery, expecting to be going home when she began running a fever and within hours became critical with blood poisoning. Mom knew it had turned serious when she saw Joe come home from the hospital and he wasn't coming to the house. She looked out the window and spied him leaning heavily against the side of the garage, weeping. Mom stayed with her her last days. When she was so very ill, Mom would tell Serene to take her prayer book and rosary and pray. Serene replied "If I do that God will want me and I don't want to die." Serene wanted to see her baby sister so Mom dressed me in a little white coat she had made and took me to the hospital. When Serene wanted to hold me the nurse said she couldn't, "You might tear your stitches, Serene." Serene then remarked, "I'll never see her grow up."

During the morning hours of November 12th, Mom went to the hall to see what time it was. Upon returning she told Serene it was three o'clock. Serene sat up in bed and sang "When it's Three O'clock in the Morning," a song they had on a record at home and was played on the phonograph. Serene knew all the words. The night Serene died we siblings were not supposed to know until Mom and Dad got home to tell us. There was a call to the neighbors and Leo "rubbered" on the phone and when he heard she had passed away, he went berzerk! Dad took it very hard, Mom was strong.

Serene passed away on Monday evening, Nov 12th, 1923. In the obituary it stated her death as 13 years, 3 months, and 7 days. She was a bright and intelligent child and always willing to do her duty at first call and all who knew her, knew her for her sweet and happy disposition.

Isabel and Grace (eighteen and seventeen years old) bathed and dressed Serene in her communion dress for burial. The services (wake) were held at the family farm in the parlor. In those days the living area was called the parlor. Classmates were pallbearers. During the visitation, a neighbor told Mom, "Her prettiest daughter died." At the gravesite when they lowered Serene into the ground all my siblings screamed, "Oh, Reeni, Oh, Reeni, Oh, Reeni!" Leo nearly lost his mind! She is buried in the Catholic Cemetery at Pine Bluff. Mom said she'd never wish her back, the world is such a cruel place!

I think Serene would have been a lot like Isabel had she lived.

Serene's First Holy Communion

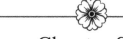

Chapter Six
Helen (Skillful Caretaker)

*H*elen was born on November 5, 1912. When she was two years old the family had scarlet fever and she was weakened so that she had to relearn to walk. Growing up she was expected to help with chores on the farm and in the house. What she hated most was mowing hay and milking cows. Helen went to Catholic elementary school full time and roomed with the sisters at the convent in Pine bluff. She completed high school, driving back and forth to Mount Horeb with Marie. (Leo spent fifteen minutes teaching Helen to drive forward shifting into first, second, third, now go! Dad taught her how to back up.) She excelled at trigonometry! After high school graduation, Dad said he was making teachers out of Helen and Marie! Helen said, "I'll be damned if I have to become a teacher!" She decided to become a nurse; I think having a ruptured appendix at the age of six and a tonsillectomy when she was a teenager had something to do with that. Imagine having your tonsils removed with only a local anesthetic while sitting in a dentist chair!!

Helen enrolled in a nursing career at St. Mary's hospital for three years. The cost was $75 a year. She took her state boards and was employed as a registered nurse at St. Mary's and did private duty. Helen's true love was surgery. There were several prominent doctors (primarily the Deans) who almost always asked for Zwettler (they called her "Zwet") as their scrub nurse for major surgeries. At St. Mary's she became acquainted with another nurse, Mildred Harrington. Down the road she would become my sister-in-law!

While nursing at St. Mary's Helen's supervisor developed an illness and had to go back to St. Louis. Before she left, Helen asked her for a nickel raise and was turned down. So she went to University Hospital with better pay. While nursing there the Deans called her to return to St. Mary's, she was that skillful!

Helen met and married Clarence "Todd" Schleck who was employed with the Northwestern Railroad. They began their married life in Tomah, Wisconsin and later moved to Dodgeville where Todd became a depot agent. They were blessed with four children: Sharon, Tom, Anne, and Joe. When Joe was four years old, Helen went back to work at St. Joseph's Hospital in Dodgeville. While the older children were in school, Todd took Joe to work with him at the Depot. Todd had to take Helen to work, she worked on the 4:00-11:00 PM shift, and then get her after midnight since Helen had no driver's license. Later on, she became employed at the nursing home where she was "Director of Nurses."

Helen lucked out marrying Todd. He was a great husband and father. He waited on her hand and foot. I never knew what that was like!

Todd and Helen retired at the same time. They sold their home and moved to an apartment on Madison's west side. They had many happy years together until Todd died of a heart attack on July 10, 1990. He is buried at Sunset Memory Gardens at West Town.

Helen continued living in their apartment on Segoe road until her health was failing in the fall of 2011. Her family put her in an assisted living apartment in Waunakee. When she needed special care she was placed in the nursing home where she died on December 10, 2014 at the age of 102. She is buried with Todd at Sunset Memory Gardens.

Helen's Baby Picture

Helen

Helen and Todd

Helen in a Persian Lambswool Coat with Sharon

Todd and Helen with Sharon and Ann

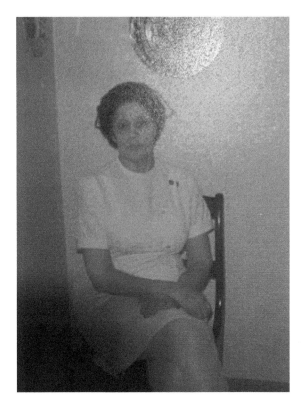

Nurse Schleck

Fred, Tom, Ann, Joe, Phil
Carol, Helen, Sharon

Chapter Seven
Marie (Adventurous Teacher)

*M*arie was born on June 27, 1914. Since she was two years younger than Helen she was also *expected to do her share of help with the family chores; milking cows, mowing hay, feeding calves, and housework which was not her way of living her teenage years. I don't recollect how she was able to attend high school after Helen graduated. Even though Helen drove them to school (you didn't need a license in those days) Marie apparently rode with neighbors.*

After graduation she attended Platteville Teachers University. In Platteville she met a very handsome construction worker. He looked like Cesar Romero and he was six or seven years older than her. She got pregnant and had the baby in Milwaukee at a Home for Unwed Mothers. She had planned to give the baby up for adoption but instead gave the baby, a little girl, to our sister Isabel who couldn't have children. Marie had named and baptized her Sheila Marie. Isabel changed her name and had her rebaptized as Mary Ellen. Isabel's husband Virgil was crazy about Mary Ellen and spoiled her rotten. She was a naughty child. For example, Isabel had swept the floor and Mary Ellen came along and kicked the dust pan on purpose. Years later, when Marie was visiting Pine Bluff, Marie told Mary Ellen that she was her biological mother. Mary Ellen was ten or eleven years old. She went right in the house to ask Isabel and all hell broke loose. There was a lot of antagonism between Isabel and Marie lifelong. I did go with Marie once to meet the biological father in Mount Horeb at Olson's restaurant. He came with another fellow and they just sat and visited. She just wanted to see him.

After one year of college you earned your degree and could apply to a school. Marie's first position was her home school, the Murphy School, with twenty or more students first grade through eighth. Prior to this first year of teaching, there were two brothers who flunked eighth grade for two or three years. Our dad was the school clerk at the time and always got the eighth grade scores and had to inform the parents if they passed. Pat and Ivan Murphy were big boys for their age and apparently school was difficult for them. When Dad got the report they had again failed, he dreaded going to the parents with the sad news. The boys pleaded, "I'm not going back." Their dad replied, "By God, you'll graduate if you have to go to school till you're eighty." Marie became their teacher and with her help they both passed!!! Needless to say, Murphys had a reason to celebrate!

After two years of building her own fires and being janitor she applied for a city school in Necedah and was hired. She always said she was tired of living out of a suitcase, riding greyhounds for home visits, and wanted to travel the country. She went to Arizona with a girlfriend, Alice Flaig, and that's where she met her future husband Robert (Bob) Barnett. He was an airport mechanic, nice looking, and six feet tall. They had two children, Betty and John, and then moved to Sacramento, California where Bob worked for the United States Postal Service. When the children were raised and were on their own, she resumed her teaching career and taught third grade in a large city school in Encino, California. She had to drive miles on the freeway. I don't know how she didn't get killed because she was the world's worst driver. She had to drive on six lanes and she could barely drive on one!

In all the years she lived in California I only remember she came home once when Betty and John were teenagers. Marie hated to fly over the mountains; needless to say, she never attended our parents' funerals. Marie died of a bleeding ulcer on April 25, 1985 in Encino and her ashes were scattered in the Pacific Ocean. Bob died of a heart attack in the fall of 1985.

There were often times I thought, "I can't see where Marie had any good in her life," until she settled in California. It's sad to think I only saw her once after she moved there.

Marie

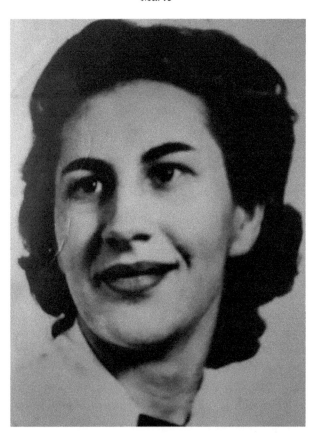

Marie

Chapter Eight
John (A Colorful Guy)

*J*ohn was born on May 17, 1917. He did the usual chores on the family farm that were expected of him. He was often hired out to the neighbors when they needed an extra hand. One such neighbor was near Riley, Bill Cuneen. He wasn't too happy working there; it was very hilly work and he had to use horse driven machinery. He wanted to go to high school but the walk a mile cross country wasn't to his liking.

In 1929, our United States suffered a terrible depression under President Hoover. President Delano Roosevelt was elected in 1932 and under his leadership the country was recovering with New Deal federal programs. I'm sure one of those programs (Agricultural Adjustment Act - AAA) saved our farm! Another operation was the CCC (Civilian Conservation Camps) throughout the United States. John signed up and joined a camp in northern Wisconsin. He worked grubbing out trees for farming and park purposes. His paychecks were sent home, saving only $5 for his own expenses. Dad and Mom saved his money and when he served his allotted time with the corps, he used this money to attend barber college in Milwaukee. After graduation he rented a shop in Madison on State Street. His business thrived enough to add another barber chair and hired Sylvester Slotten from Bellville. As fate would have it the building was sold. He was told to pack up his belongings and get out. He went down the street and commiserated with a friend who told him, "That's small potatoes! I own an empty building and you can set up shop there!" So he created a barber shop in Cambridge. He had a great business when war broke out with Japan!

He had a beautiful girlfriend, Claire, that he dated for quite a few years. Claire expected a diamond every Christmas and never got one. After five or six years she broke it off, the love affair ended. He did buy her a beautiful diamond but it was too late. She had met someone and was going to be married.

Japan bombed Pearl Harbor and President Roosevelt declared war against Japan. There immediately was a draft for men to serve and John volunteered to join! John was in the Medical Corps with the 5th Army, served time in Africa and from there to Sicily, Italy right in the thick of battle with Germany. He was with the hospital on the front lines and saw many wounded soldiers. At one time he was ordered to dig a fox hole but instead jumped in one with his captain who wasn't too pleased! He told John " I expect a good many free haircuts." He also worked part time in the kitchen and made friends with the Italians nearby. He would sneak food, mainly summer sausage, to poor families- in return he was given wine and the best 100 proof cognac which he shared with the soldiers and officers in camp. He did date a nurse there which was a no-no because she was an officer!

The war ended in May 1945 against Nazi Germany when they surrendered. Adolf Hitler committed suicide on April 30th with his lover Eva Braun. Victory in Europe Day was declared on May 8th. On September 2nd, Japan surrendered following the atomic bombings of Hiroshima and Nagasaki. The fighting finally over, the boys could come home and John was happy to be a civilian again! He lived at the farm for many weeks but stayed dressed in his army garb. He was hesitant to talk about what he had seen on the front lines. I was dating Jack Harrington at the time and when John saw how nice Jack looked in dress clothes he immediately went shopping and returned to civilian life. John was home for Thanksgiving when Mom decided she wanted turkey for dinner instead of chicken. Dad bought one at the local turkey farmer, Bob Kirch. What a wonderful family gathering that was! Mom's sage dressing was absolutely delicious!

After Thanksgiving, John began his barber business in Madison, renting a barber shop again and adding two more chairs. At this time Leo made the move to Washington and wanted John to join him but he refused. He was enjoying the good life- wine, women, and song! He was the most colorful of all the family! Every Sunday, he brought a host of friends from Madison to the farm. Mom always had plenty to eat. Then after dinner we'd all play Red Dog. I always sat beside John because he would cover my bets. Once I had three aces and a king covering all the suits. I showed him my hand and he told me to bet the pot - $80!! The other *ace turned up and he had to cover the bet. Everyone at the table was absolutely shocked.*

One time, a professor of human studies with the University of Wisconsin came into John's barber shop and just sat watching him...ALL DAY! He then commented how well John could converse on multiple topics, weather, sports, politics, etc. with his customers. He told John, "That's exactly what I teach!"

John met and was infatuated with Lois Ireland of Waunakee. She was a renowned artist and had studied abroad. They married in April of 1958 and moved to Oconomowoc, again with his own barber shop. Lois knew all about Claire and didn't mind that he would meet her for dinner between Madison and Milwaukee once in a while to catch up.

John and Lois had two sons, Scott and Chris, who excelled in school and graduated from the University of Wisconsin-Madison- both in engineering degrees. Chris lives in a suburb of Minneapolis with his wife Julie and has horses. Scott lives in another suburb of Minneapolis with wife Sheila, two children, Jack and Rose. Both Scott and Chris were engineers for companies in the twin cities.

John and Lois lived in the outskirts of Oconomowoc and in 1994 John's health was failing and was hospitalized several times at the Veterans Hospital in Milwaukee when he died on Feb 12, 1995. Funeral services were held at a Catholic church in Oconomowoc and burial the following day in Ixonia with only the immediate family attending. It was very disappointing to John's family that he did not have a military service after all his years in the army. He certainly was deserving of the honor. When John died, Claire sent me a letter saying she fondly remembered all the beautiful dinners at the Zwettler farm.

Lois sold her home and moved to Hastings, Minnesota to live near her sons where she lived in an assisted living apartment. Lois contracted COVID-19 and passed on December 30, 2020.

John

The following are several photos of John in the Service

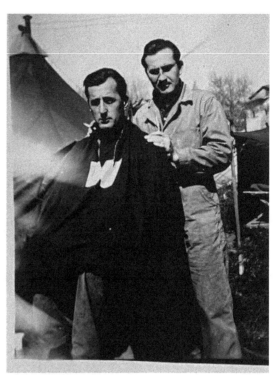

Lois

Photos of John and Lois

Lois, Chris, Joseph, Mary, John and Scott

33

Chapter Nine
Bernard (Master Storyteller)

*W*hen Bernard was born on August 19, 1919, Mom was at a loss for a name for the newborn. As fate would have it, Grandpa Florian Zwettler was spending a few days on the farm and overhearing Mom searching for a name, he said "Mary, Bernard is a nice name." Hence Bernard Matthew was born. His teenage years were a great help on the farm. Farming in those days were drudgery times- using horse drawn machinery to plant crops- harvesting the hay crop was extremely hard work, but Bernard was always a willing hand. Recreation time was spent playing baseball, training horses for riding, making their own skis for winter pastime, and in the fall cutting wood for fuel in the winter. He only went one week to high school!

Playing baseball in their spare time really helped them to join Home Talent Leagues. Bernard and Ray played for Pine Bluff and Cross Plains. Hyland, a menswear store in Madison, sponsored a Riley team and they would play at Breese Stevens Field in Madison, a big ballpark on the east side of Washington Avenue. One night their farm team played the University of Wisconsin Ball Club and trounced them- 28 to 8!!

Bernard was a third baseman and Ray played first base! Bernard said he played the hot corner! Connie Grub, an ace pitcher who played on the Ashton Home Talent (later played professional for the Washington Senators) told me at Bernard's wake he always hated to pitch to Bernard "because he could never strike him out." He was a fast runner and never failed to tell how he stole from third base to home plate and scored!

When President Roosevelt declared war against Germany and Japan in 1941, Bernard joined the Army before he could be drafted. He was placed in the infantry as a runner and reported to Portland, California. In wartime a runner had to take instructions from one base to another. After many days of training he developed pain in his ankle from an old injury. (While cutting wood with his dad and Ray, the ax accidentally slipped off a chunk of wood and sliced into his ankle. He was taken to Mount Horeb to be stitched up. He never complained about it.) Because of the lingering pain and discomfort in his ankle, he was taken to the commissary and the doctors wondered how he ever passed his physical. They immediately determined he was not a soldier they wanted on the front lines. They ordered an Honorable Discharge and sent him home. He pleaded with the officers to enter the cavalry because he knew how to handle horses but it was to no avail. Their reply, "the army wants no part of you! Your injury is too severe for any active duty." He had no alternative but to go home and farm again with Dad. He was very handsome and chased after by many girls! One in particular was Joan Harrington, later my sister-in-law. After dating several years they became engaged, set a wedding date, and two weeks to the "big day" he called it off. I don't think anyone ever knew why. I surmised it was because money he was going to receive from Dad to renovate the old house went to a different sibling.

When Bernard found out he was to have gallbladder surgery, he and Isabel drove out to our farm to consult with me about how I recovered from mine. I told him it was a piece of cake. So when I went to see him after his surgery he was suffering with lots of pain. He told me, "It was no @#$%^^ piece of cake!!!"

Bernard went to work for Frank Gabelt around MIneral Point on Highway 14 building roads. During the workday, he suffered a severe pain in his head that was disabling. Frank called Ray and then the ambulance which took him to St. Mary's Hospital in Madison. It turned out to be a cerebral hemorrhage. This was a latent result of a car accident that happened much earlier.

Bernard had driven his parents and Uncle Pete to visit relatives in Kansas. When reaching Kurtsville, Missouri, they were hit broadside. Mom broke her collarbone, Bernard hit his head, and Dad and Uncle Pete weren't injured. Mom was the only one hospitalized. Isabel was called and IMMEDIATELY she and Ray drove to the hospital. While in the hospital an insurance man visited Mom and told her, " Mrs. Zwettler, we're going to owe you a lot of money!" There was a jury trial and Dad had to testify. Mom was awarded $25,000!

Mom and Dad enjoyed another visit to Chanute, Kansas to visit Aunt Rose Wheeler, her son Ernie, wife Mabel, and daughter Lena. Aunt Rose was a lovely lady and it was sad to learn she had a child when young that was given to Mom and Dad to raise. My sister, Isabel remembered Albert as an adorable dark haired little boy. Albert died of spinal meningitis when he was six years old and is buried somewhere in Monroe, WI.

On this same trip they went on to Tulsa, Oklahoma to visit another daughter, Edna, and her husband, John. Edna didn't know about a little brother, Albert, until Bernard told the story. Isabel was furious with him. To make matters worse, while they were there, John died suddenly! Edna eventually moved back to Chanute.

In 1948 Mom's health was failing. A woman was hired to help in the kitchen but then it was decided to sell the farm and move to Madison. That was a sad day for Bernard! He found employment as an agricultural farm hand for the University of Wisconsin. One of his jobs was taking care of baby calves. He often said he knew more about tending them than the vets that were hired by the University! He lived with Dad, Mom, and Isabel on Sprague Street in Madison. During this time Edna had moved to Madison, Wisconsin where she worked in a dime store on the square. She moved into the house on Sprague Street to be with family.

We all loved to listen to Bernard tell stories. Once while visiting our farm in Arena, he was telling quite an embellished one and stood up to be more effective. Isabel rolled her eyes and said aloud, "Oh God, he's standing up, now we're going to get it!" He was a wonderful storyteller, always had rapt audiences!

When Bernard reached retirement age he bought land near Verona and built a log cabin home and bought a sawmill. He went into business sawing lumber. When Mom died, Edna moved to the log cabin to care for Bernard. In his spare time, he enjoyed going to the Greyhound Race Tracks in Dubuque and Wisconsin Dells. On July 18, Bernard and a friend, Walter Zweifel, and I attended the Greyhound races at the Dells. We stopped in Sauk City on the way home and enjoyed a lovely dinner at a local restaurant, Likstreu. On the next morning, July 19th Bernard died suddenly of a heart attack. It was so traumatic for all the family. My daughter, Joan, came home with a chicken to cook for all gathered there. She, Jane (another daughter), and I decided we should clean up the gravesite so it would look nice the day of the burial. We bought some flowers on the way but forgot planting tools! We had to stop at a tavern called Rettemunds to borrow the needed tools from Terry. We will always remember how kind and helpful he was on such a sad day. It turned out to be a big funeral with so many family members, co-workers, ball players and it seemed all of Pine Bluff! He looked so handsome in the casket....his eyebrows were jet black. As you look back, it's funny what little details you remember. He is buried in the St. Mary's Catholic Cemetery in Pine Bluff alongside our parents, sister Serene and Grandma Bergen. Bernard would be happy to know he is buried in the beautiful hillside. He had a military funeral and Ray was given his flag.

And Edna moved back to live with her sister, Lena, in Kansas.

Bernard

Schmitz, was built and then abandoned during World War II when there weren't enough young men to field a team. The diamond was rebuilt after the war.

There may not have been baseball in Pine Bluff during the war, but at least some of the Pine Bluff men were playing baseball. Barney Zwettler was one of them. In 1941 he was playing second base at Fort Ord, Calif. "There were 37,000 men in camp and nine baseball teams. I made the No. 1 team," he said.

Barney and his brother, Ray, both were on the early Pine Bluff teams.

in Eau Claire. The Army ended that career," Barney Zwettler said.

Barney is a retired farmer. Ray is a retired timber buyer. Schmitz, who also played on the first Pine Bluff team, runs a Pine Bluff tavern with his wife, Rosie.

Barney Zwettler remembers the crowds that used to turn out for a Pine Bluff game. "One Sunday we had a crowd of 8,000," he said. "We played a Madison team called Pat's Tigers and we beat them, 7-4."

Turn to Page 17, Col. 1

Blaine Krantz   Joe Schmitz   Wayne Brink

Barney Zwettler   Harold Krantz   Ray Zwettler

Chapter Ten
Raymond (Charming Ballplayer)

*R*ay was born on June 27, 1921. He was a cute blond haired baby- what a contrast next to three older dark haired brothers. He had a sweet disposition and was always good natured, but at times could also be very mischievous, often playing tricks on his baby sister... teasing her about the "boogie man." There was always plenty of work to do on the farm, mainly in the fall. Dad had a grape and apple orchard and it was our responsibility to pick the apples off the trees, fill the bushel baskets that Dad would place by the roadside for the neighbors to enjoy- free of course! He had many varieties, snow apples, delicious, Greenings, etc. The Delicious apples he would store for the winter buried in the oats bin in the grainery- they never froze and always stayed crisp until spring. And with the grapes he made wine.

Ray did graduate high school and was a good student. He excelled in the manual arts. He played football and baseball. One time he fell off his horse and hurt his ankle but played baseball that night anyway. He went to the doctor the next day and found out it was broken! Now that's mind over matter!

For recreation we played cards- Spades, Hearts, Euchre, Old Maid, and Monkey (Spoons). Like Bernard he excelled in baseball; played in the Home Talent Leagues first base and caught. He was a homerun hitter. In 1940 he won a trophy for the lead hitter of all the league. In 1941 he had a tryout for the Milwaukee Braves, made the team, and trained in Arizona. Again war intervened in 1942 with Nazi Germany and Japan. He left the ball club and went home. Because boys were being drafted for the army, the Draft Board deferred him as a farm laborer so he was exempted from serving in the war.

On May 17th, 1949 he married Doris Keller, a beauty from Belleville and bought a tavern in Pine Bluff. They had four boys- Joe, Dave, Doug, and Van then finally a daughter Serene. Serene was a Down syndrome baby and Doris wasn't told immediately following the birth. Ray was told and was down the hall from the hospital room when he heard Doris scream. It was a difficult realization but life is what you make it. Serene was raised with her brothers and she brought a lot of joy to their lives. She now resides in a group home in Reedsburg.

With a hired bartender, Doris managed the tavern in the daytime and Ray helped at night when he was home. He was a timber buyer for Hiram Walker out of Prairie du Chien - their main products were whiskey barrels. When the business was sold, Ray received a severance check and began his own business; buying and selling logs for logging companies.

Ray and Doris decided a tavern was no business to raise a family so they bought a farm in Plain. Their sons and daughter attended school in Spring Green in the River Valley School System. After graduation the boys left home to attend college and find employment. Joe and Dave attended Whitewater College, Doug went to Denver, found employment with a gas and electric company. Van was adventurous and ended up in Boise, Idaho.

With her sons on their own, Doris decided she wanted to work outside the home. She applied at the nursing home in Reedsburg and was employed as head cook. She was very clean, polishing her shoes white every day and was a great homemaker. She had to leave her job in the fall of 1993 when she developed diabetes. In the spring of 1994 she had a severe sore on her right leg and had to have an amputation below the knee. Ray and the help of her sister Eve changed bandages and took care of her until September when Ray suffered a heart attack and died on the way to the hospital. He had services at St. Luke's Catholic Church in Plain. One of Ray's close friends, Dr. Zauft, just could not attend the funeral, it was too sad. He had played ball with Ray for many years in Sauk City. A week after his funeral, Helen and I had tickets to go to Denver to see Helen's daughter, Ann. That trip saved me, I think.

Five weeks later Doris developed a painful sore on her left foot, was hospitalized and her doctor had her scheduled for surgery until they discovered her heart was failing and could not survive the operation. She *died on October 18, 1994 and was also buried from St. Luke's. They now are laid to rest in a beautiful hillside in the Plain Cemetery. Ray was not only my revered brother but my best friend. I miss him terribly.*

Ray

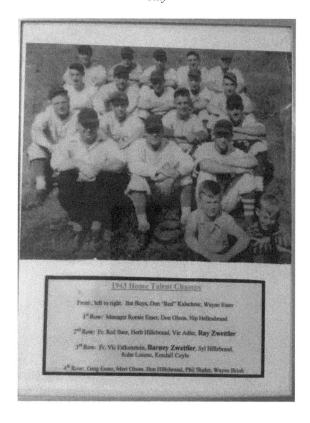

KEEP GIVING

YOUR NEW BREWERS OF 1946

PITCHERS	B	T	Ht.	Wt.	Age	Winter Address	Club 1945	W	L	Pct.
ACOSTA, JULIO	L	L*	[illegible]	[illegible]	[illegible]	Havana, Cuba	Milwaukee	14	10	[illegible]
BALSER, LEON	R	R	[illegible]	[illegible]	[illegible]	Cleveland, Ohio	Nat'l Def.			
*[illegible], BOB	R	R	[illegible]	[illegible]	[illegible]	Kenosha, Wisconsin	Nat'l Def.			
BLOCK, [illegible]	R	R	[illegible]	[illegible]	[illegible]	Milwaukee, Wisconsin	Semi-pro			
BURKART, ELMER	R	R	[illegible]	[illegible]	[illegible]	Baltimore, Maryland	Milwaukee	2	3	[illegible]
BURKE, DELVAN	R	R	[illegible]	[illegible]	[illegible]	Milwaukee, Wisconsin	Semi-pro			
CARLSON, CLIFFORD	R	R	[illegible]	[illegible]	[illegible]	Grand Rapids, Michigan	Nat'l Def.			
CHRISTENSEN, JACK	L	L	[illegible]	[illegible]	[illegible]	Duluth, Minnesota	Nat'l Def.			
CROWLEY, JERRY	R	R	[illegible]	[illegible]	[illegible]	Milwaukee, Wisconsin	Nat'l Def.			
[illegible], JAMES	R	L	[illegible]	[illegible]	[illegible]	Mosinee, Wisconsin	Nat'l Def.			
DAWSON, DONALD	R	R	[illegible]	[illegible]	17	Janesville, Wisconsin	Semi-pro			
DAVIS, WENDELL	R	R	[illegible]	[illegible]	[illegible]	Kansas City, Missouri	Milwaukee	[illegible]	[illegible]	[illegible]
DEL CALVO, OSCAR	L	R	[illegible]	[illegible]	[illegible]	Havana, Cuba	Portsmouth	[illegible]	[illegible]	[illegible]
*EISENACH, BOB	R	R	[illegible]	[illegible]	[illegible]	Milwaukee, Wisconsin	Nat'l Def.			
[illegible], FRANCIS	R	R	[illegible]	[illegible]	[illegible]	Gary, Indiana	Semi-pro			
[illegible], DON	R	R	[illegible]	[illegible]	[illegible]	Waukegan, Illinois	Nat'l Def.			
JANISZEWSKI, RAY	L	L	[illegible]	[illegible]	[illegible]	Cudahy, Wisconsin	Middletown	[illegible]	7	[illegible]
JOHNSON, MILO	R	R	[illegible]	[illegible]	[illegible]	Watervliet, Michigan	Nat'l Def.			
[illegible], EDDIE	R	R	[illegible]	[illegible]	[illegible]	Chicago, Illinois	Nat'l Def.			
KONETZKE, ED	L	L	[illegible]	[illegible]	[illegible]	Menasha, Wisconsin	Semi-pro			
LANFRANCONI, WALTER	R	R	[illegible]	[illegible]	[illegible]	Barre, Vermont	Nat'l Def.			
LINDE, LYMAN	R	R	[illegible]	[illegible]	[illegible]	Beaver Dam, Wisconsin	Nat'l Def.			
LINDQUIST, CARL	R	R	[illegible]	[illegible]	[illegible]	Emporium, Pennsylvania	Milwaukee	[illegible]	[illegible]	[illegible]
LIVENGOOD, WES	R	R	[illegible]	[illegible]	[illegible]	Winston-Salem, N. C.	Nat'l Def.			
MARINO, FRANK	R	R	[illegible]	[illegible]	[illegible]	Chicago, Illinois	Nat'l Def.			
NOLAN, MATHEW	L	L	[illegible]	[illegible]	[illegible]	Minneapolis, Minnesota	Middletown	[illegible]	[illegible]	[illegible]
PYLE, EWALD	L	L	[illegible]	[illegible]	[illegible]	Du Quoin, Illinois	Milwaukee	[illegible]	[illegible]	[illegible]
[illegible], FREELAND	R	R	[illegible]	[illegible]	[illegible]	Oakfield, Wisconsin	Semi-pro			
[illegible], STEVE	R	R	[illegible]	[illegible]	[illegible]	Chicago, Illinois	Nat'l Def.			
SCHEETZ, OWEN	R	R	[illegible]	[illegible]	[illegible]	Columbus, Ohio	Milwaukee	[illegible]	7	[illegible]
TROTTER, BILL	R	R	[illegible]	[illegible]	[illegible]	Fairfield, Illinois	Rochester	9	13	[illegible]

CATCHERS	B	T	Ht.	Wt.	Age	Winter Address	Club 1945	Bat. Ave.
*[illegible], SAM	R	R	[illegible]	[illegible]	[illegible]	Elmwood Park, Illinois	Nat'l Def.	
DENNING, OTTO	R	R	[illegible]	[illegible]	[illegible]	Chicago, Illinois	Milwaukee	[illegible]
EDWARDS, GENE	R	R	[illegible]	[illegible]	[illegible]	[illegible], Wisconsin	Milwaukee	
FERNANDEZ, MANUEL	R	R	[illegible]	[illegible]	[illegible]	Tampa, Florida		
GRISWOLD, HARRY	R	R	[illegible]	[illegible]	[illegible]	Long Beach, California	Nat'l Def.	
HEATH, TOM	R	R	[illegible]	[illegible]	[illegible]	Clovis, California	Nat'l Def.	
*KOPPA, CYRIL	R	R	[illegible]	[illegible]	[illegible]	Wausau, Wisconsin	Nat'l Def.	
[illegible], JOHNNY	R	R	[illegible]	[illegible]	[illegible]	Chicago, Illinois	Nat'l Def.	
[illegible], STEVE	R	R	[illegible]	[illegible]	[illegible]	Sharpsville, Pennsylvania	Middletown	[illegible]
PADDEN, TOM	R	R	[illegible]	[illegible]	[illegible]	Manchester, N. H.	Milwaukee	[illegible]
[illegible], JOE	R	R	[illegible]	[illegible]	[illegible]	Detroit, Michigan	Semi-pro	
RADDANT, KEN	R	R	[illegible]	[illegible]	[illegible]	Shawano, Wisconsin	Wilkes-Barre	[illegible]
[illegible], JAMES	R	R	[illegible]	[illegible]	[illegible]	Milwaukee, Wisconsin	Nat'l Def.	
[illegible], RAY	R	R	[illegible]	[illegible]	[illegible]	Mt. Horeb, Wisconsin	Semi-pro	

INFIELDERS	B	T	Ht.	Wt.	Age	Winter Address	Club 1945	Bat. Ave.
BRAINARD, DAN	R	R	[illegible]	[illegible]	[illegible]	Sanford, Florida	Nat'l Def.	
[illegible]	[illegible]	[illegible]	[illegible]	[illegible]	[illegible]	[illegible], Kentucky	Middletown	[illegible]
GILLESPIE, EARL	L	L	[illegible]	[illegible]	[illegible]	Green Bay, Wisconsin	Nat'l Def.	
[illegible], JOE	R	R	[illegible]	[illegible]	[illegible]	Park Ridge, Illinois	Nat'l Def.	
KAMZIC, NICK	R	R	[illegible]	[illegible]	[illegible]	Chicago, Illinois	Nat'l Def.	
[illegible], ART	L	L	[illegible]	[illegible]	[illegible]	Chicago, Illinois	Middletown	[illegible]
McWHORTER, MACK	R	L	[illegible]	[illegible]	[illegible]	Mobile, Alabama	Nat'l Def.	
MOORE, LLOYD	R	R	[illegible]	[illegible]	[illegible]	Pomeroy, Ohio	Nat'l Def.	
NAGEL, BILL	R	R	[illegible]	[illegible]	[illegible]	Memphis, Tennessee	Chicago AL	[illegible]
NIEMANN, JOHNNY	R	R	[illegible]	[illegible]	[illegible]	Chicago, Illinois	Nat'l Def.	
POLITO, VINCE	R	R	[illegible]	[illegible]	[illegible]	Lancaster, Pennsylvania	Vol. Retired	
REYNOLDS, DAN	R	R	[illegible]	[illegible]	[illegible]	Martinsville, Virginia	Chicago AL	[illegible]
[illegible], JOE	R	R	[illegible]	[illegible]	[illegible]	Eau Claire, Wisconsin	Portsmouth	[illegible]
[illegible], TOM	R	R	[illegible]	[illegible]	[illegible]	Wauwatosa, Wisconsin	Nat'l Def.	
VINCK, RAY	R	R	[illegible]	[illegible]	[illegible]	West Allis, Wisconsin	Nat'l Def.	
WALLA, BARNEY	R	R	[illegible]	[illegible]	[illegible]	Baltimore, Maryland	Nat'l Def.	

OUTFIELDERS	B	T	Ht.	Wt.	Age	Winter Address	Club 1945	Bat. Ave.
BURGO, BILL	R	R	[illegible]	[illegible]	[illegible]	Windber, Pennsylvania	Milwaukee	[illegible]
CARROLL, CHUCK	L	L	[illegible]	[illegible]	[illegible]	Brookfield, Illinois	Middletown	[illegible]
*DELSING, JIM	L	R	[illegible]	[illegible]	[illegible]	Stevens Point, Wisconsin	Nat'l Def.	
EPPS, AUBREY	R	R	[illegible]	[illegible]	[illegible]	Memphis, Tennessee	Nat'l Def.	
FERNANDEZ, AURELIO	R	R	[illegible]	[illegible]	[illegible]	Havana, Cuba	Williamsport	[illegible]
FLICK, LEW	L	L	[illegible]	[illegible]	[illegible]	Kingsport, Tennessee	Milwaukee	[illegible]
JOHNSON, BOB	R	R	[illegible]	[illegible]	[illegible]	Yelm, Washington	Boston, NL	[illegible]
[illegible], THOMAS	R	R	[illegible]	[illegible]	[illegible]	Johnson City, New York	Nat'l Def.	
[illegible], TONY	R	R	[illegible]	[illegible]	[illegible]	Cicero, Illinois	Milwaukee	[illegible]
NICHOLS, FRED	R	R	[illegible]	[illegible]	[illegible]	Jackson, Alabama	Nat'l Def.	
*[illegible], VINCE	R	R	[illegible]	[illegible]	[illegible]	Chicago, Illinois	Nat'l Def.	
*[illegible], BOB	R	R	[illegible]	[illegible]	[illegible]	West Allis, Wisconsin	Nat'l Def.	
VANHOFF, HAROLD	R	R	[illegible]	[illegible]	[illegible]	Spokane, Washington	Middletown	[illegible]

*Denotes player still in service.

Doris

Ray and Doris

Doris, Serene, Van, Ray
Joe, Dave, Doug

Leo, John, Ray, Bernard, and Todd

Chapter Eleven
Eileen

*O*n June 20, 1923 the last of the clan joined the family of Joseph and Mary Zwettler. All through my teenage years I was labeled as being "spoiled." Perhaps I was! How could I have not been "special" with all my brothers and sisters at my every beck and call! Isabel and Grace took care of me when I was born. One time John was standing beside the crib and patting me and Mom said, "Don't hurt her Johnny." He replied, "I'm just making her tame!" However, I was never shown any leniency when it was chore time. Our duties were many: feeding chickens, gathering eggs, helping hay, milking cows, mowing the lawn, keeping the woodbox filled by throwing chunks of wood into the basement for fuel, and then all of the household duties. I enjoyed painting the rooms and was always proud of my beautiful home and farm.

Ray and I would walk to Catholic School in the fall and spring. In the winter we'd walk or get a sleigh ride to the Murphy country school one mile away. Once an elderly woman (in her sixties) became a long term substitute at the Murphy school. She didn't have any discipline and there were several unruly students. Dad was clerk of the country schools and one of the neighboring Laufenberg boys told him how terribly she was being treated. Dad asked who the trouble makers were and Ray and I were on the list. Dad had to take care of the problem so he walked to the Murphy School with the razor strap and all we had to do was see him and we straightened up! The Laufenberg boy was hiding under the school's porch when he saw Dad coming.

In remembering the activities my brothers were involved in, I think I was a "tomboy." I had to do everything they did. They made their own skis and even made ski jumps. They had riding horses and of course I had to learn how to ride, Lindy was my favorite. I knew how to put on the bridle and saddle and ride bareback at a young age. Lindy galloped like the wind, and I loved it! When the men were too busy to get the cows at milking time, I would saddle Lindy and gather up the cattle from the pasture. They could be miles from the barn. Lindy would even have to jump a creek, which was often scary.

The scariest time in my life was when I swallowed a thumbtack! I was eleven years old and I was standing at Mrs. Conrad's desk at the Murphy School and spotted a tack on her desk. I picked it up and I don't know what behooved me to put it in my mouth and I accidently swallowed it! When I told the teacher what I had done she made Ray and a friend, Clifford, walk me home- about a mile. They told Mom and she was just floored! She took me to the neighbor's next door, Martha Martinson, because I was wheezing and Martha said, Get her to a doctor!" We went to Dr. Thompson in Mount Horeb and had to climb a steep stairway to the second floor. He took one look at me and wouldn't treat me. I had to go to St. Mary's and see Dr. Tormey. When he listened to my chest, he didn't like what he heard and scheduled surgery for the next morning. We had to stay overnight in Madison at Charlie and Margaret Meicher's an old neighbor from Pine Bluff that now lived in Madison. I was in surgery for a couple of hours the next day as the doctors tried to remove it with a bronchoscope that had a magnet. I started to turn blue and they had to stop. I had to rest overnight at the hospital and the doctors attempted to remove it again the next day, but failed. A priest came to see me, Fr. Zuern and I asked him if I was going to be ok. He tried to lighten the mood and said, "We are never OK until we have our tonsils and appendix out." I added, "And false teeth!"

My sister, Helen, was a nurse but wasn't allowed in the operating room, however she hovered right outside the doors. When on the third try they got the thumbtack up as far as my throat she went running down the hall screaming, "They got it , they got it." What she didn't know was that it fell off and it took some time before it was finally recovered. I do remember being wheeled down the hall and seeing all the brilliant lights *streaming overhead. I was also told at one point it took many in the room to hold me down. When it was over, Dr. Tormey came to see me and he asked whyever did I do such a thing and that I was lucky because some cases like this ended up being transferred to Philadelphia! My Mom prayed throughout and promised she'd give her diamond ring to a religious organization if God would let me live! She did send it!*

In elementary school at the end of the school year all one room schools got together at one site to have a playday. When I was in eighth grade it was in Black Earth. I entered every running race - gunny sack, three-legged, potato relay, etc. and got several blue ribbons beating out my rival, Alice Williamson.

I loved my high school years! As a freshman I tried out for the cheerleading squad and made the team, hence it was four years of fun. Then our sports were mostly football and basketball. In 1941, my senior year, our basketball team went to state. I was a cheerleader at the fieldhouse in Madison. We won the first game, but lost the second.

Carlton Midthun was a dear high school friend. He was expelled for smoking on school grounds. I formed a petition to have him reinstated with over one hundred signatures and sent it to our principal. During the eighth period when all grades were present in the main hall, Principal Wendt came to where I was sitting in the sixth row. All eyes were watching him as he leaned his elbow on my desk and said, "Eileen, I'm surprised by that petition from one of our leaders!" I responded, "Mr. Wendt, everyone deserves a second chance!" Carlton was back in school the next day!

The president of the junior class was always the prom king. When I was a junior it was going to be Milton Showers. He was a great guy from Blue Mounds and had a car to drive to Mount Horeb. He was sweet on me and another girl, Myrtle Martinson. I was sure he was going to ask me to be his queen, so I turned down a few other offers from classmates. I had a good friend in Home Economics, a class taught by our junior advisor. Unbeknownst to us was Mrs. ??? had asked Milton to meet with her after school. My friend was working on a project after school in the Home Ec room when Milton walked in and Mrs. ??? asked directly who he was going to ask to Prom. He told her, "Eileen Zwettler." She told him he had to ask Myrtle because she was from Mount Horeb! I was shocked but still wanted to go so I asked a good friend, Art Post, to take me. He had been out of school a couple of years but was happy to do so. The theme was "Gone With the Wind" and my sister, Helen, offered to let me wear a beautiful green formal of hers. I felt just like Scarlett O'Hara as I walked into Prom!

One of my favorite classes was typing/shorthand. At the age of ninety-nine, I can still take dictation in shorthand!!

In my senior year of high school I had to live in a rooming house in Mount Horeb. There were no school buses in those days and I had no way to get there otherwise. I had a charge account at a local grocery store. It was called the Royal Blue Store. And if I needed money I only had to ask Mr. Nelson for cash! I was the envy of my roommates!!!

After graduation, I would often help my sister Grace at the restaurant she was managing at the time. It was on Monroe Street in the vicinity of Edgewood. When America was at war in World War II many munitions plants were built throughout the country making many different kinds of war equipment. One such plant was built in Madison on East Washington Avenue. It was called "R&R" where they made walkie talkies. I got a job there as an inspector. This company often employed servicemen home on leave. I would often punch additional time to their timecards because of their service to our country. One of them was a good friend, Sheldon Hollopeter. He ended up working at my table. He would often ask me to go on coffee breaks with him. He wasn't handsome but nice-looking and I enjoyed his company. He asked me to go to a Badger basketball game and we took a cab. I was stunned when he was shipped off to England overnight and I never heard from him for a long time.

In the spring of 1942 I was making enough money to buy a fur coat. It was $800 to be exact and it was on sale! It was a conversation piece my whole life. I dated Jack Lucey (my brother-in-law's nephew), a cute lieutenant in the army, around this time. He told his family he liked me because I wasn't a giggly teanager. I wrote to him in Iran and would go out with him when he came home on leave. I recall going to a dance at Spanish Village with him and wearing my fur coat. Boy, did I think I was something!

Shortly after Christmas in 1943, a neighbor girlfriend came home with her army husband. They were stationed near Indianapolis. Hazel persuaded me to go back with them which I did and immediately got an office job at Curtis Wright airplane factory. While working there I attended part time at the IBM School of Accounting in bookkeeping. A friend, June, and I would often go to a roller skating rink for recreation. We were pretty good! There was also a huge roller coaster that we tried. I never would ride one again! I was never so scared in my life!

Then in July, Mom became ill with pernicious anemia and I had to return home. She fought this illness for years. Finally the doctors determined she needed vitamin B shots weekly. Isabel and Helen were able to give them to her every Sunday for years.

In the fall of 1945, I met my future husband. I had been on a double date with Stanley Halverson, Stanley's sister, and my brother, Ray. We'd been to a dance at the Riverside Ballroom in Sauk City and stopped for a bite to eat at the Greasy Spoon. There were two vacant seats at the horseshoe counter so we girls sat down. I happened to sit beside Jack Harrington. We got visiting and he found out my cousin, Mary Sawle, was his neighbor! I think he was a little smitten right away because the next day he went down to Sawles' and wanted Mary to set something up. The following Saturday night I went down to a dinner at Mary and Sam's and there was Jack. After dinner we went dancing at the Riverside. We dated almost every weekend from then on. He was farming for his father in Arena at the time. Besides dances we went to family gatherings and enjoyed playing cards with friends. Jack had many friends! One time, we walked into a local restaurant/bar called Governor's and there was an open seat next to.... Jack Lucey! I sat down and we began visiting. I always had to drag Jack H. away from his friends but this was one time he came to me and said he thought we should get going!

Jack and I dated for about a year and I was given a diamond on my birthday in June. Jack was always a gentleman! Papa, Jack's dad, said he wore out a car dating me but he thought a lot of me. Mama, Jack's mother, was furious when he bought a diamond for me because she wanted him to give me hers!

After I was engaged, I was at the home farm varnishing french doors and a car drove in from Ohio. It was Pete Hollopeter and a friend. They ate supper at the farm then took me to a bar in Madison. He asked me for a favor, he wanted to give me a kiss. He was a nice fellow, always respectful. After I was married, Pete would call Isabel wondering how I was doing.

Jack and I were married on November 30, 1946. It was a full day of activities. A breakfast for the family that Mom made, the wedding, the dinner back at the farm that Mom and neighbor ladies cooked, and then a wedding dance in Cross Plains. We rented a nearby small house that was just up the road from his family farm for $13 a month. His take home pay was $100 a month and we shared a car with his parents. After Mary, our first, was born in 1948 my mother went to speak with Jack's folks about splitting the cost of our hospital bill. Mama refused. By the time we had two children, Mary and Steve, it was not easy making a living under those conditions. I exerted pressure for Jack to take over the farm. Papa and Mama were willing to sell so we went to Wiinch's law office in Mazomanie to draw up the papers. They wanted $20,500 but I asked Papa how much they had paid- $18, 500. They reconsidered and we bought the personal property for $18,500. His parents moved to Madison and rented an apartment near Madison General Hospital where Papa got a job as a janitor. As it turned out, Papa would come home for lunch and he often wouldn't go back, so he got fired.

One of the first things we did when we moved to the bigger farmhouse was to install a stoker. This auger would feed the coal into the furnace in the basement so I didn't have to continually go outside, open the heavy basement doors and down to feed the furnace manually. Mama and Papa had looked into installing a new boiler piping heat throughout the house but it was going to cost one thousand dollars so they didn't have it done. One good thing about shoveling the "klinkers" (coal chunks too large to process) out of the furnace grate was they were then thrown outside on the driveway to be traction for the milk truck hauling our milk cans.

I tried to be a helpful farm wife but there were a few occasions when I caused a bit of grief! Putting hay in the topside of the barn was an ordeal. I drove the Farmall tractor that was attached to a huge long rope.

The rope went through a pulley that raised and lowered the hay fork carrier used to grasp piles of hay. I couldn't see Jack and just had to listen for his directions. Well I drove too far and broke the rope. He wasn't very happy with me so I jumped in the car and drove to Patron's Mercantile in Black Earth and bought him a 100 foot rope. On another Sunday morning we were putting hay into the barn and I wasn't doing anything right so I shut off the tractor and walked to the house. I told Jack to put his own blasted hay up!

One day we had a cow that calved on the hillside and we had to go get her and her calf. We took the truck and put the calf in the back then the cow would follow us home. Jack told me NOT to drive in the direction of the slough but I ended up going that way and got stuck. Jack put his elbows on the hood of the truck and said, "I have a #$%% good notion to shoot you!" I had on brand new white tennis shoes but I got out and pushed to get that truck out!

We belonged to St. Barnabas Catholic church and were very involved. At one time, Jack was president of the Parish Council and I was on the funeral lunch committee. I had to work at the funeral of Mike Lucey and Jack knew my old boyfriend would be present. Jack Lucey did come sit beside me while we lunch ladies had our dinner. We enjoyed a long visit. Later that afternoon I was home refinishing a dresser and my husband, Jack, drove into the driveway. When he got out of the truck he said, "I suppose you saw your old boyfriend today!" I answered, "Yes, we had a long visit!" Talk about adding fuel to the fire! He was only ever jealous about him.

I've undergone several major surgeries during my lifetime, suffering with gall bladder difficulties was terribly painful. I suffered a serious gallbladder attack when I was pregnant with Jane and had to be hospitalized and on an IV for four days. My sister, Helen, thought I passed a stone even though X Rays didn't show stones. A few years later, I had to have a hysterectomy and during that surgery the surgeon felt gallstones! Helen insisted I have my gallbladder removed and had it scheduled. The day before the surgery, Jack and I took our children (four at that time) to the Dane County Fair. On the way home, Jack dropped me off at St. Mary's for surgery the next day. Helen took Nancy and Tim to stay with her family in Dodgeville while I was hospitalized. The day I was discharged, Jack was thrashing so I had to take a cab to Isabel's on Sprague Street in Madison. The cab driver had to carry my luggage up the steps as I was too stooped over and in so much discomfort. Mom took one look at me and said," Eileen, you shouldn't be out of the hospital!" I rested. Isabel came home from work at University Hospital and made supper. Then she and Mom took me home out to the farm. Isabel didn't like to drive the main roads so took all back roads. Every bump we went over jarred the incision and My Lord that hurt! What I didn't know was the men were thrashing at our farm. The neighbor ladies had come to put fresh linens on the bed and Doris Zwettler (Ray's wife) had done all the cooking for the thrashers! She was a saint cleaning up the kitchen and helping me settle.

Jack's six sisters at this time were all living in Madison with the exception of his sister Helen and she lived in Wooster, Ohio. Believe me, having six sisters-in-law was not what I envisioned for my married life but I think I handled it with fortitude and grace.

We also acquired the neighboring farm for $48,000 but after quite an ordeal. We had lovely elderly neighbors, the Sheehans, who wanted to sell us eighty acres of their land for $16,000. I didn't think it was worth that much and told Jack we had to decline. They were lifelong neighbors and Jack just couldn't do it. He made me go with him and I just told Mr. and Mrs. Sheehan that we had some bad news, we couldn't afford the land at that particular time. As it turned out it was fortunate because a short time later another neighbor wanted to sell his six hundred acre farm that adjoined ours. Harold Roberts always liked Jack and was newly remarried. His new wife said she'd stay on the farm for a year and it ended up being only a month. She wanted to move to Sauk City. Harold really hoped we would be interested. We bought that farm for $48,000 at 1% interest. It is where our son, Steve, and his wife, Linda, raised their family and still reside.

Jack and I have six children: Mary, Steve, Nancy, Tim, Jane and Joan. Mary worked for many years at the Department of Transportation in Madison. She has three children - three grandchildren and resides in Sauk City. Steve and Linda (Moe) have three children - seven grandchildren. Nancy and Jane graduated from Platteville University. Nancy married Dick Harker, taught a number of years and lives on a farm in Mineral Point. They have three children - two grandchildren. Jane married Paul Hess, worked in social work and lives in Edgar. Tim studied for a year and half at Platteville and then returned to farm with Steve. Tim married his high school sweetheart in August of 1979 and took over the family farm. They have two children. Jack and I built a house between the two farms. Jack and I sold the farms to the boys and they formed a partnership called the Harrington Brothers. Joan graduated from the University of La Crosse and went on to Dr. Scholz School of Podiatry in Chicago. She and her Husband, Scott Kjar, have a podiatry practice in Platteville where they live.

When Joan was in her senior year of high school I applied for a job at Greenway Manor where I worked until I retired in 1982. I loved my job in housekeeping. My first task was learning how to operate the buffer. It was a heavy cleaning machine for the hallways and I lost control of the thing and it put a great big hole in the drywall! Everyone thought it was a big joke and never let me live it down. After practicing a bit more I could run it using one hand! As I look back I drove to work in some very inclement winter weather! There were times Jack told me to stay home but I went anyway thinking the place couldn't run without me. I was pretty chummy with most of the staff but especially the Director of Nursing. We'd go out to lunch and I would comment that I felt out of my league around her and the nursing staff. She told me that I meant as much to her as her nurses. Wasn't that kind!

I've had the good fortune of visiting several states with family members - Kansas, Georgia, Ohio, Colorado, Minnesota, and Iowa. When I worked in Indianapolis, my friend June lived in Evansville, Indiana so she drove me over the state line so I could say I'd been in Kentucky. I've always wanted to go to the Kentucky Derby but never made it there. I took the Amtrak to Seattle but it was after Leo had passed and I flew with family to Ireland when I was eighty-seven! We went on a bus tour with around fifty others from various states and made great friends. The scenery, people, attractions and entertainment was unmatched!

Life took a very sad turn in January of 1992. Jack became ill with a heart problem and on February 15, 1992 he died in his sleep. He had a large Irish funeral at St. Barnabas Catholic Church in Mazomanie and is buried in the cemetery there.

As I am writing this at the age of ninety-nine I am residing in my hillside home that Jack and I built. I am in good health but have macular degeneration in one eye and glaucoma in the other. I am still able to play cards and watch television. It was very difficult not being able to read books by my favorite authors, do cryptoquotes, or put together jigsaw puzzles but I adjusted.

As I am ending this Zwettler journal I hope you enjoyed reading as I certainly have enjoyed writing it.

I remain sincerely yours,
Eileen Zwettler Harrington.

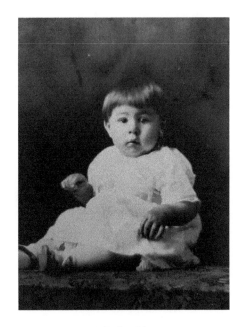

My Baby Photo

My First Communion and Leo

Zwettler, Eileen
"Kelly"
"Let's laugh and
sing and be gay."

Girls' C. 2,3,4
G.I.S. 4
Dramatic C. 1,2
Pep C. 1-4
Cheerleader 1-4
Camera C. 4
Glee C. 3
Card. Highs. 4

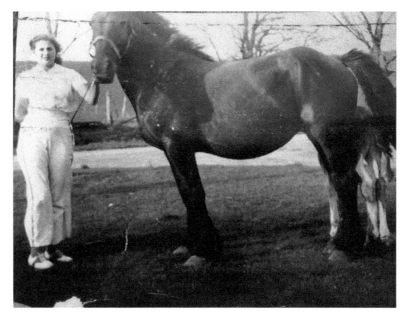

With Lindy, My Horse

Our Wedding in 1946 at St. Barnabas Catholic Church in Mazomanie, WI.

Our Twenty-Fifth Wedding Anniversary
We held a dance at the Riverside in Sauk City, WI

1977

Bernard, Ray and Me

Helen, Me, Isabel on a trip to Georgia to see Grace

Playing Cards
Todd, Helen, Leo, Ray (back to camera), Bernard, and Me

Joan, Nancy, Mary, Jane
Tim, Me, Steve

Mary, Jane, Joan, Tim, Nancy, Steve

Tim, Nancy, Steve, Jane
Joan, Me, Mary

Playing and Winning at Cards!!!

Anecdotal Stories

Story of Aunt Theresa Zwettler and Aunt Bertha Bergen

Aunt Bertha lived at home with her parents, Peter and Rosina, and siblings, Mary, Pete, Casper, and Rose. Joe Gabalt was a friend of the family and was in love with Aunt Bertha and asked her to marry him. She refused, telling him, "Marriage is not for me!" Joe Gabalt then left Wisconsin and settled in South Dakota.

Now, my dad's sister, Aunt Theresa was CRAZY about Joe Gabalt so she went to Aunt Bertha to ask if she would ever change her mind about him. Bertha firmly said, "No, Never!"

Theresa then followed Joe to South Dakota pursuing him and eventually they married. They had four children: Florian, Frank, Joe and Mary. (Mary married Samuel Sawle and I ended up being her neighbor when I married Jack.)

Joe and Theresa returned to the Pine Bluff area and during the 1930s, Joe contracted the flu and was dying. Theresa walked three miles to a tavern in Pine Bluff to call the doctor. On the way she remembered she'd left a burning candle in Joe's hand (religious offering) but was too far along to turn back. The doctor really couldn't do anything for Joe and he died a few days later. My dad then bought Theresa, his sister, eighty acres of land in Pine Bluff.

Uncle Pete (Mom's brother)

Uncle Pete rented an eighty acre farm in Riley and the property only had a small house and barn. His crops were always the last to be harvested, I think because he'd have a celebration. Uncle Pete would set up bales outside for seating and would get a keg of beer. Mom and I would place a washtub outside with a basket of towels so the farmers could clean up. Thrashing was dirty work! We'd also wash all his silverware beforehand to be sure it was clean. I'd go with Uncle Pete in his Model A Ford to Klevenville to get crackers, cheese and bologna to serve the crew.

Little House - "Poor house"

When our family moved to the big house, our little house became vacant. Andrew Brink was on the board for homeless and needy people. There was a family in Mount Horeb that required assistance. They had four sons and one daughter with no employment and were dirt poor. Andrew contacted Dad to see if they could live in the little house. They lived there until they found a home in Blue Mounds. One of the sons developed appendicitis and went to the hospital. He was left in the hallway while they took other patients because he was a county patient and didn't have insurance. He died in that hallway!

The second family to occupy the little house was a widow with two children. The son had a job but the daughter lived with her mother. A neighbor's hired man was "sparking" the daughter and was caught trying to sneak into the house by the mother!!

At one time the little house became "Beecher's Tavern". Mom got a phone call at 2AM from a woman looking for her son and his friends. Dad had to get up, dress, and go across the road to check in the tavern and there they were! Off they quickly went on their way home!

History From a Radio

My dad just adored Franklin Roosevelt! I can remember him sliding his chair up close to the radio listening to the Fireside Chats. FDR covered so many topics of concern to the American people from the late thirties into the early forties: the bank crisis, New Deal programs, Works Relief Program, unemployment, inflation, the coal crisis, the progress of WWII, etc. Leo would leave Seattle and come back to Wisconsin every three years. He'd bring cigars and sidle up with Dad to listen to history. And Dad's sister, Sister Isabel, would love to stay with our family at the farm because Mom catered to her- fresh starched linens, hot water in her room in the morning, delicious meals and even a beer once in a while. She would enjoy time spent with Joe beside the radio.

Some Marriages - A Wonder

In the neighborhood lived a handsome elderly widower with seven sons. A neighbor girl kept house for them and she was crazy about one of the sons. This son had gone to the seminary to become a priest but left and went back home. He couldn't see her for dust so she went to be a maid in Madison. This son missed her housekeeping so he started dating her in Madison. I came home from Indianapolis one weekend and heard they were planning a wedding! After Mass, I went with others to Schmitz's Tavern and ran into the old widower and I told him how happy I was for his son and soon to be daughter-in-law. With tears in his eyes he responded, "He doesn't love her, Eileen, he's just marrying her for a housekeeper!" Well, the couple raised a family and her mother lived with them their whole married life! They stayed together but whether they had a happy marriage is a wonder!

Kindly Neighbor

There was a young bachelor living on our road when I was in my early twenties and engaged. When I'd drive by I'd always wave to him. Low and behold, there was a beautiful canister set given to us the day of our wedding. It was from the kindly gentleman.

Hospital Visitors

I had a tubal pregnancy...Thomas Whalen, married to Jack's aunt (Rose), wanted to come see me. Aunt Rose and their son, Tommy didn't want to go, Thomas got on the bus from Ridgeway to the Madison bus station. Once there, he called a cab to take him to St. Mary's Hospital to visit me. He must have thought a lot of me!

Fr. Ireland was a very handsome priest, the son of another of Jack's aunts (Nell). He would come to Madison but he couldn't stay with his mother. He'd stay with the chaplain at St. Mary's Hospital. He came to visit me while I was a patient there. During our visit he happened to say, "My mother has me so busy visiting the fallen away Catholics!"

Father Ireland

In the fall of the year, I happened to be busy cooking cranberries on the stove with my back to the door and I heard the porch door open. I just thought it was Jack when suddenly Fr, Ireland bent over and kissed me on the cheek! He often would come out to the farm with Mama, Jack's mother. They chuckled over my surprise. They were still there when the school bus dropped off our children. Tim came into the house first and Father said, "Give your mother a kiss, you are never too old to kiss your mother!"

When we got the call that Papa, Jack's dad, had passed away on November 24, 1958. I said we had to go to Madison to see Mama. Joan, Jack's sister, was there. I asked if Fr. Ireland knew and no one had called him. When Joan contacted him in Florida he flew to Madison and officiated the funeral service. I walked in and sat with the grandchildren during the funeral. One of Jack's uncles, Bill Kelly, asked Mama, "Where did Junior (Jack) find that lovely woman?" I guess Mama answered, "If we'd searched the whole world over we'd have never found anyone nicer!" I can't believe Mama said that!

Father Ireland loved icicle pickles. On the way out to their car to return to Madison, Mama whispered to me, "Go get one of your jars of icicle pickles for Father!" You'd have thought I'd given him a million bucks!!

Apple Trees

Growing up on the farm in Pine Bluff we had around fifteen apple trees. When the apples ripened all of us kids would be up in the trees picking and putting them in bushel baskets. After Mom had canned what she needed, all the extra bushels of apples were put beside the road with a sign that said "FREE". They always disappeared and we were happy to help others.

After I was married, we had apple trees on the Arena farm too. I happened to be sewing a brown suit for myself when Jack came into the house and said it was going to freeze over the evening so those apples better get picked. I went out and got on a ladder and picked and picked all the apples. Let me tell you, Jack had apples for breakfast, lunch and dinner for two weeks!

Compliments

Jack was always very complimentary about how I looked, outfits I made or how I fashioned my hair. There were a few haircuts, however, when he didn't say a thing and then I knew they weren't flattering. There were a few hats that I ended up giving away too. They were the ones with feathers, he disliked birds.

Jack and I were out with friends, one being Donald Murphy. I happened to remark how pretty Alice Lindley was. Donald said, "Have you ever looked in a mirror!" That was pretty sweet!

I was all dressed up to go out with Jack to a dance. Tim was about six years old and he looked up at me and said, "You're so beautiful, how could any man resist you!"

Family Favorite Recipes

APPETIZERS

Oriental Cocktail Meatballs
1 ½ pounds ground beef
¾ cup rolled oats
1 can (5 oz) water chestnuts, drained and chopped
½ cup milk
1 egg, slightly beaten
1 tablespoon soy sauce
1 teaspoon MSG
½ teaspoon each, garlic salt and onion salt
¼ teaspoon salt
Dash of hot pepper sauce
Shortening for frying
Sauce: Combine all ingredients except shortening and mix thoroughly. Shape into balls, using tablespoon of mixture for small ones, 1 teaspoon for miniature ones. Brown in small amount of fat in a large skillet. Drain off fat. Prepare sauce. Yield: 4 dozen small or 8 dozen miniature meatballs.
Sauce:
1 can (8 ½ oz) crushed pineapple
1 cup firmly packed brown sugar
2 tablespoons cornstarch
1 cup beef bouillon
½ cup (or less) vinegar or lemon juice
2 teaspoons soy sauce
½ cup chopped green pepper

Drain pineapple, reserving juice. Mix brown sugar and cornstarch in a sauce pan. Gradually stir in pineapple juice, bouillon, vinegar and soy sauce and cook, stirring constantly until it is thickened and clear. Stir in green pepper and pineapple. Pour sauce over meatballs. Simmer for about 10 minutes for small meatballs and 5 minutes for miniature. Serve hot with picks.

Pickles With Grape Leaves
Put a grape leaf, little garlic & onion in a jar. Put in cukes & dill. Make brine of:
1 cup water
1 cup white vinegar
2 Tbsp. salt
1 Tbsp. sugar
Bring to boil & pour over the cukes. Put a grape leaf on top of cukes – seal

Popcorn Balls
4 qts popped corn
2 cups coarsely chopped pecans

1 cup butter

1 1/3 cups sugar

½ cup light corn syrup

1 tsp vanilla

Mix first 2 ingredients in a large pan

Melt butter in a small heavy saucepan and add sugar and corn syrup.

Bring to boil – stirring until simmer – 3 min

Add vanilla and nuts. Pour over popcorn, mixing constantly

Dampen hands with cold water, shape into balls

Sausage & Velveeta on Rye Bread – Doris Zwettler

1 # hamburger

1 # sausage

Brown with onions, drain

Melt 1 block Velveeta cheese, add 2 Tbsp. oregano, garlic salt

Add to meat, spread on Rye bread & freeze on cookie sheet. Store in the freezer!

Braunschweiger Pate – Doris Zwettler

1 lb braunschweiger

2 pkg green onion dip mix

1 tsp sugar

2 tsp water

1 Tb Lawry's Garlic spread

1 8 oz size cream cheese, softened

1 Tb water

1/8 tsp Tabasco sauce

Mash braunschweiger. Combine dip mix sugar & 2 tsp. water. Blend in sausage. Form into igloo shape and plate. Chill. Melt garlic spread. Whip cream cheese, water & Tabasco. Blend in melted garlic spread. Spread over braunschweiger like frosting. Chill & serve with crackers.

Mustard – Winnie Sawle

1 tsp. mustard

½ tsp. salt

1 Tbsp. sugar

1 Tbsp. flour

1 tsp. melted butter or olive oil

1 Tbsp. vinegar

Chunk Pickles

7 lbs. cucumbers

3 lbs. sugar

1 pt. vinegar

1 oz. allspice (whole)

1 oz. celery seed

1 oz. stick cinnamon

Cut cucumbers in about 1 inch lengths and use 2 c. salt to 1 gal. water. Soak for 3 days and drain. Let stand in clear water for 3 days and drain. Stew in half vinegar & half water and alum, the size of a walnut for 2 hrs. Boil syrup for three min, pour over pickles hot – that have been packed in jars.

Ice Cream
1 qt. milk
4 egg yolks
¾ cup sugar
½ tsp. salt
3 heaping T. flour

Cook above and add:
1 cup whipping cream
1 cup Pet milk (evaporated milk)

SOUPS & SIDES

Frozen Cabbage Salad
¾ cup w. vinegar
1 cup powdered sugar
½ tsp salt
1 tsp celery seed
Boil 5 min
Shred cabbage – sprinkle with salt. Let stand ½ hour – if juicy, drain – add chopped peppers, onions – mix with syrup & freeze!

German Potato Salad – Ada Roelke
1/2# bacon, cubed & fried. Put through a strainer & save crispy cubes. To drippings add 1 c vinegar, 1 c water, 1 c sugar, 4 tsp. salt, freshly ground pepper, ½ tsp. paprika, bring to boil. Mix ¼ c cornstarch in ¼ c cold water. Add to boiling brine & cook till slightly thickened and glassy. Slice potatoes while still warm & add finely chopped onion

California Cheese Soup
1 quart boiling water
2 chicken bouillon cubes
1 c diced celery
½ c diced onion
2 ½ c diced peeled potatoes
1 c diced carrots
1 bag (16 oz) frozen California blend veggies
2 cans cream of chicken soup
1 lb Velveeta cheese
Add all veggies to boiling water & bouillon cubes. Boil 'til tender.
Then add cans of cream of chicken soup and Velveeta, stir 'til melted.
Salt & pepper to taste

Marinated Carrots
2# carrots – peel & quarter. Boil 10 min, drain & cool
Sauce:
1 can tomato soup
¾ c sugar
1 c vinegar

1 tsp. salt

tsp. prepared mustard

dash horseradish

1 TB Worcestershire sauce

Layer carrots, onions, peppers. Pour sauce over & leave overnight

Potato Salad Dressing

1 c. vinegar

1 c. sugar

1 tsp. dry mustard

1 stick butter

4 egg yolks, beaten

½ tsp. salt

1 Tb. flour

In a saucepan, beat egg yolks and vinegar. Mix sugar, salt, dry mustard and flour well and add to the vinegar mixture. Add butter. Boil (and stir) until thick. Cool. Add mayonnaise (if needed).

DESSERTS

Caramels (Aunt Sugar's)

2 cups white sugar

1 ¾ c white Karo syrup

1 can sweetened condensed milk (Carnation)

2 sticks of butter

Blend all ingredients in heavy kettle (scorches easily)

Let come to a hard boil – stirring constantly

Simmer until mixture forms a hard ball in cold water – stirring occasionally

Add 1 cup walnuts and paraffin (wax) size of quarter

Pour on a greased cookie sheet.

Let cool – cut into pieces while still somewhat warm then let to get hard

Wrap in wax paper

Coconut Dessert

1 T sugar

1 c flour

½ c butter

8 oz cream cheese

1 c powdered sugar

2 pkgs coconut pudding

1 pkg Cool Whip

3 c milk

Combine first three ingredients, add nuts (optional) – pack in 13"x9" pan

Bake at 350°, 15 minutes – cool

2nd layer – mix cream cheese, powdered sugar and fold in 1 cup cool whip – spread on crust

3rd layer – cook pudding with milk – spread on above
4th layer – top with rest of cool whip

Ginger Snaps
cream: ¾ c Crisco
1 c sugar
Add and beat well: ¼ c dark molasses
1 egg
Sift together: 2 cup flour
2 t baking powder
1 t cinnamon
½ t cloves
½ t ginger
½ t salt
Roll into balls – roll in sugar
Bake at 375° for 8 to 10 minutes – less for a soft cookie!

Cinnamon Candy
1 cup of water, bring to boil. Remove from heat, add 2 cups sugar, ¾ cup light corn syrup, 1 tbsp of butter, return to heat, bring to boil, now cover with lid about 3 minutes, now uncover and boil until crispy when dropped to cold water, then add ½ teasp. of cinnamon and a few drops of red food coloring. Butter cookie sheet.

German Chocolate Cake Frosting
1 c evaporated milk
1 c sugar
3 egg yolks
½ c butter
1 tsp vanilla
a. Combine above in saucepan – cook over medium heat until thick (about 12 minutes)

1 1/3 c coconut
1 c pecans

b. Stir in; heat until thick enough to spread

Surprise Carrot Cake
2 c unsifted flour
2 tsp baking soda
2 tsp ground cinnamon
½ tsp ground ginger
½ tsp salt
3 eggs
1 ½ c sugar
¾ c mayonnaise
1 can (8 oz) crushed pineapple in juice, undrained
2 c coarsely shredded carrots
¾ cup coarsely chopped walnuts

Grease and flour 2 (9") round baking pans. In a bowl stir together the first 5 ingredients, set aside. In a large bowl with a mixer at medium speed beat the next 4 ingredients until well blended. Gradually beat in flour mixture until well blended. With a spoon, stir in carrots and walnuts. Turn into prepared pans. Bake in a 350°F oven 30 to 35 min or until a cake tester inserted in the center comes out clean. Cool in pans for 10 min. Remove, cool. Fill and frost with 2 cups whipped cream.

Brownies – Ruby Turnell
2 cups sugar
2 T Karo syrup (use dark)
4 eggs
1 cup shortening
4 sq. chocolate
1 ½ cups flour
½ tsp. Baking powder
2 tsp. Vanilla
nuts

Mix the first 3 ingredients. Add melted shortening & chocolate. Add flour, baking powder, vanilla and nuts. Put in a large cake pan. Bake for 20 min. (or longer) at 350°. Frost as soon as you take it from the oven.

Frosting
2 cups powdered sugar
4 T. cocoa
4 T. butter
4 T. hot coffee
½ t. vanilla

Rhubarb Shortcake
Line a baking pan 9x13 with rhubarb (4 cups). Cream 1 ½ c sugar & 6 T butter. Then add 1 cup milk, 2 cups flour, 2 tsp. baking powder & ½ tsp. salt – mix well & pour over rhubarb – Top with topping mix:

1 ½ c sugar
½ tsp salt
2 Tbsp cornstarch

Sprinkle over batter – Pour 2 cup boiling water (add red coloring if desired) over entire mixture – Bake 1 hr, 375°

Blueberry Dessert
Crust: ½ cup butter (or oleo)
½ cup sugar
1 ½ cups graham crackers, crushed

Press into about 9x9 pan or bigger

Filling: 1 pkg. 8 oz. cream cheese, little salt, ½ cup sugar – mix well
Add 2 eggs that have been well beaten, to the above mixture. Spread over the crust that has been pressed into tin. Cover the whole thing with 1 can (about 1 lb, 6 oz) blueberry pie filling. Bake for 25 min. at 350°. Place in the refrigerator to cool. Serve with whipped cream. (May add blueberries after cooked)

Lemon Poppy Seed Cake

1 box (18 ½ oz) lemon cake mix
4 whole eggs
¾ c vegetable oil
1 box (5 ½ oz) instant vanilla pudding
1 ¼ c cold water
½ c poppy seed
1 can (21 oz) lemon pie filling
1 pint whipping cream – sweetened with 1 tsp sugar, 1 tsp vanilla

Combine dry cake mix, eggs, oil, dry pudding, water & poppy seeds. Mix well with the mixer – about 4 minutes. Bake at 350° in a 9x13 pan – cool. Spread lemon pie filling on cake. Frost with whipped cream. Refrigerate at least 4 hours before serving.

Sour Cream Raisin Pie

1 c raisins
½ c sugar
1 tbsp. flour
1 tsp. cinnamon
½ tsp. nutmeg
¼ tsp. salt
1 ⅓ dairy sour cream
3 egg yolks, beaten
1 tbsp. melted butter or margarine
1 tsp. vanilla
Pastry for 1 crust (9") pie
Meringues:
3 egg whites
6 tbsp. Sugar
Pour hot water over raisins; let stand for 20 minutes. Drain.
Combine raisins with sugar, flour, cinnamon, nutmeg and salt.
Add remaining ingredients and blend until smooth.
Pour into the pastry shell. Bake in a hot oven(400 degrees) for 10 minutes.
Reduce heat to slow oven (325 degrees); bake for 45 minutes.
Cool and top with meringue.
Meringue: Beat three egg whites to soft peak stage. Slowly add 6 tbsp sugar and beat until stiff peaks form.
Spread on pie; brown in moderate oven (350 degrees) 10 to 12 minutes.

Poppy seed Noodles - as dictated to Jane by Mom (Eileen) when she was 99 years old!

   For as long as Mom can remember, she had this traditional Austrian dish every Christmas Eve. Her mother, Mary, made the noodles Christmas Eve day and it took all day to be ready to eat at supper and then again after midnight mass. The noodles were served with prune sauce. (Papa, her dad, always thought the bread noodles were constipating and prunes helped!) That was the whole meal! You couldn't eat meat on Christmas Eve. She doesn't know how Mama did it – especially on a wood stove! The tricky part was immersing the noodles in hot water just to moisten being very careful not to soak the noodles to soggy. Every pan was used and they were all over the kitchen!

There wasn't a Christmas that her brother Leo wouldn't write home missing family and THE NOODLES. (Mom often thinks of Leo on Christmas Eve and how lonesome he must have been.) One Christmas Eve

Mama, Mom's mother, was watching the neighbor's 3-yr old little boy, who looked at the noodles and blurted, *"Dem's dirty."* Another Christmas Eve on the way home from a cousin's house and supper, Papa spoke a truth too, *"Noodles were like bullets"* – Mom's noodles were THE BEST! Everyone in the family liked the noodles EXCEPT for Helen's husband – he, Todd, didn't like and famously said, *"Thank God for the coffee, it helped!"*

Mom vividly remembers poppy seed noodles starting at age 8 (1931) because that was the same year she learned there was no Santa Claus – *"the lights went out for me"*! She thought neighbor, Leo Meicher, was Santa Claus because he always visited at Christmas, making the family kneel down and pray the Our Father and Hail Mary prayers.

On to the famous recipe –

1. Bacon grease will be needed at the very end of the recipe. Get frying!
2. Roll bread dough to small 1/2" balls. Let rise to double in size about 1 – 1 ½ hours.
3. Meanwhile heat poppy seed (about 10 oz) in the microwave 15 seconds to help the opium oil and enhance flavor. (Remember as you do this that Mama used the wood stove.)
4. Grind the poppy seed with a coffee mill until the texture is clumpy and the color turns from black seed to whiter like salt and pepper.
5. Add sugar to the ground poppy seed – ½ c sugar to 1 c poppy seed (depending on how many noodles you make).
6. After the dough has risen, BAKE at 325 for 20 minute or until bread balls are light brown and done.
7. Get pans of water boiling because water must be hot. Here's the TRICKY PART – immerse the baked bread balls into the hot water just to get the noodles moist. This step won't take long. Use a spoon to stir noodles in the hot water. Avoid soaking for too long which gets noodles soggy. Drain in colander.
8. In a big bowl, roll noodles in the sugared poppy seed mixture.
9. Heat bacon grease to piping hot. Pour grease over noodles, a little at a time, while stirring to completely cover.
10. Serve warm. *"They're delicious!"*

Acknowledgements
By Nancy Harrington Harker

This book has been on quite a journey. The stories traveled their way through many family members and friends to be included. My siblings (Mary, Steve, Tim, Jane, Joan) have their favorite stops, as do I. For historical references, I looked to our family historian, Steve Harrington, and his binders of family information. His contributions were significant and gave the family adventure real clarity.

I was fortunate to have a high school guidance counselor who was a master at her profession. Mrs. McCutchen advised me to register for Typing I and chemistry. I did neither and on many occasions regretted not mastering typing!! Thankfully, I enlisted the aid of two of our three children, Abby Fernan and Justin Harker. Matthew, you would have been included had you been available but I also worried what details you might have added!

Jane Hess contributed many thoughtful ideas and enjoyed the task of writing (and tasting) the process of making poppy seed noodles - a family favorite for **most** of us! Several cousins - Ann Stevenson, Sharon Esch, Doug Zwettler and Scott Zwettler - joined in this venture sending information and heartwarming pictures of relatives loved and lost.

We owe Em Hughes, Executive Publisher and Alyssa W., Managing Editor at New Book Authors Publishing a great deal of gratitude in agreeing to tackle this project. Thank you to all those mentioned; this has been a labor of the heart. The final words of gratitude are for our mother.

Mom, you are an inspiration to us and all that have had the privilege to know you. You are graced with poise, determination, patience, and curiosity. Throughout your lifetime, you've been daughter, sister, cheerleader, a patriot working in the R & R and Curtis Wright factories (we can't believe you still recall "shorthand"), farmwife, mother, grandmother, great-grandmother, nurse, cook, baker, teacher, seamstress, crafter, church worker, caretaker for the elderly, sports backer and fan, champion card player, a forceful Democrat, and now author! We stand in awe of you and your incredible memory. Your stories will continue to inspirit others; we couldn't be more proud!

We love you!!

Mary, Steve, Nancy, Tim, Jane and Joan

CPSIA information can be obtained
at www.ICGtesting.com
Printed in the USA
BVHW010928110723
667065BV00022B/1575